I Found It on the Internet

COMING OF AGE ONLINE

FRANCES JACOBSON HARRIS

AMERICAN LIBRARY ASSOCIATION

Chicago   2005

Design and composition by ALA Editions in Electra and Futura using QuarkXPress 5.0 on a PC platform.

Cover photographs: *Top*, University Laboratory High School (Urbana, Ill.), yearbook photographs, various years; *bottom*, University Laboratory High School, contemporary photograph by the author.

Printed on 50-pound white offset, a pH-neutral stock, and bound in 10-point cover stock by McNaughton & Gunn.

The paper used in this publication meets the minimum requirements of American National Standard for Information Sciences—Permanence of Paper for Printed Library Materials, ANSI Z39.48-1992. ∞

Library of Congress Cataloging-in-Publication Data

Harris, Frances Jacobson.
    I found it on the Internet : coming of age online / Frances Jacobson Harris.
        p.   cm.
    Includes bibliographical references and index.
    ISBN 0-8389-0898-5
    1. Libraries and teenagers. 2. Internet and teenagers. 3. Internet—Social aspects.
  4. Internet—Moral and ethical aspects. 5. Computer network resources—Evaluation.
  6. Information literacy—Study and teaching. 7. Information technology.
  8. Communication and technology. I. Title.
    Z718.5.H38 2005
    025.04–dc22   2004030119

Printed in the United States of America

09 08 07 06 05   5 4 3 2 1

CONTENTS

ILLUSTRATIONS

PREFACE

Back in the fall of 1987, during my first week on the job at the University of Illinois at Urbana-Champaign's University Laboratory High School, two boys climbed out of a library window onto our aged second-floor balcony and proceeded to bombard the students below with water from their high-powered squirt guns. At that time the library had one computer, which we booted up from a cassette tape player. It connected us to a regional union catalog that students searched using a command line interface to find books in our library. Today, our students are just as likely to bombard one another with virtual flames (i.e., angry or inflammatory e-mails and instant messages) as they are with actual water. In the library, they now have access to multiple full-service computer workstations, all with high-speed Internet access and links to a wide variety of user-friendly catalogs and databases. Clearly, many things are different now than they were in 1987 (or 1967 or 1947, for that matter). Our tools and systems have changed dramatically. But other things are not so different. The teenagers who use the tools and systems are still teenagers.

As a school librarian for almost twenty years and an academic librarian for eight years prior to that, I have seen many exciting developments in information and communication technology. I have also seen how teenagers have altered their modus operandi as a result of growing up with these new technologies. The popular press has focused on problems that arise from the controversial digital content that teens can now easily get their hands on, including pornography and hate literature. But the focus on content misses the point by oversimplifying the complex issues that are involved. In my experience, the problems that arise as a result of communication technology are just as serious as those spawned by information technology. What teens do to one another online and the uses they make of technology for personal and social development are issues that have not received the attention they deserve.

Perhaps this lack of attention is due to the fact that, for the most part, adults do not use information and communication technology to the extent that teenagers use them. I concur with the assessment of Marc Prensky, who calls today's students "digital natives," that is, native speakers of modern digital languages who "think and process information fundamentally differently from their predecessors" (2001, 1). Adults are, at best, "digital immigrants." No matter how well-versed we become in the language, we will always retain our accents. In the classroom and in the library, digital immigrants and digital natives operate on different time clocks. Digital immigrant teachers hold on to sequential structures of instruction—lectures, step-by-step lessons, "tell-and-test" approaches—but their native audience thrives on multitasking and immediacy.

Many digital immigrants believe that digital natives have short attention spans precisely because of all their pointing and clicking. But perhaps natives *choose* not to pay attention because their immigrant instructors do not make lessons worth paying attention to compared to everything else they experience. On the other hand, when have teenagers paid attention when they did not feel like paying attention? Most teens interact with today's technology tools in profoundly different ways than their elders, but fundamentally, teenagers can still be counted on to behave like teenagers. While we must respond to the importance of digital technologies in their lives, we cannot ignore the people they are inside, as well as the people they are becoming.

As institutions, libraries have not stood still in response to the technology tidal wave. The library used to mean "The Library"—a physical structure, a place to store books, a destination. Almost all the information within it had been vetted and selected. Teaching library use was a matter of explaining the organization of resources and the various search protocols and rules. Now, in an information world that seems anarchic, the instructional work of a librarian is part Sherlock Holmes and part Indiana Jones. Where we used to point out the differences between magazines and journals, we must now also teach that there is a difference between fraudulence and honesty, between mindless ranting and erudite punditry. Only then can we begin to talk about such traditional nuances as the differences between self-publishing, editorial review, and peer review.

Librarians are also becoming ethicists and counselors. The increasing confluence of information and communication technologies has permanently altered the nature of a career once focused primarily on information organization and retrieval activities. Teens use the technologies as much for personal development as for the purposes intended by their inventors. Librarians must heed the negative ways teens choose to use the technology at their disposal, as well as the unpleasant experiences they may endure at the hands of others who wield that technology. It is no longer sufficient to teach our well-worn lessons on intellectual property rights and plagiarism. Now we must also educate students to protect themselves online, as well as to become responsible users of information and communication technologies.

This book examines the significance of coming of age in a world in which access to online information and communication tools is a fact of everyday life. I explore the impact of this phenomenon and what it means to librarians and teachers, addressing thorny underlying issues in ways that I hope will help us think not only about *what* we do but also *why* we do it and where we want to go next. Such musings are now possible because, at least on good days, the technology finally works. We have moved beyond the most painful stages of testing and troubleshooting our systems. Internet access no longer grinds to a halt when an entire class tries to go online at the same time. Now we need to decide how best to deploy this technology in support of learning in our institutions.

We have already come a long way. Our professional literature is replete with how-to manuals for teaching with technology and running technology-based libraries. But we still must come to terms with the way kids perceive the world as a result of growing up with digital technology. They experience a ubiquitous connectedness that was impossible to imagine even ten years ago. By listening to teens and learning from their native perspectives, we stand a much better chance of harnessing the power of technology in ways that enhance core library services and systems. In turn, one of the most important things we can do as professionals is to continue modeling and teaching what we know. As librarians and educators, we are in a position to provide the kind of direction and structure that teenagers need to navigate the murky waters of modern technology. We will succeed by working *with* teens rather than *for* them (or even despite them), as partners and collaborators in retooling and invigorating our vision of library services for the future.

ACKNOWLEDGMENTS

There are many people to thank when it comes to the preparation of a book. I cannot begin to name all those who have had a hand in helping me with this endeavor. So let me just say *thank you*, in the loudest possible voice, to the individuals who have been so generous with their time and thoughts. I would like to deliver particular words of thanks to the following folks:

The students of University Laboratory High School, without whom there would be no book. Thank you for your insights, your generous responses to my questions, your insatiable curiosity, and your never-ending ability to make me laugh. I have learned more from you than I can say.

The University of Illinois at Urbana-Champaign for granting me a semester-long sabbatical to work on this book. The University Library (my "boss") for arranging staffing at my library during my absence. Graduate assistants Robin Mittenthal and Lori Kunc, for teaching my classes, maintaining our website and the computers, and keeping the students well-entertained. Lisa Janicke Hinchliffe, for taking time away from her duties at the University Library to watch over things. Runelle Shriver, for being the essential linchpin, who managed the library and did the real work while I sat at home in front of my computer.

Christine Jenkins, my sabbatical partner and friend, for many hours of discussion, feedback, and inspiration. Betsy Hearne, first for urging me to write this book, then for volunteering to read my manuscript. Pauline Cochrane, for her painstaking care in explaining the idiosyncrasies of the cataloging world to me and for being so passionate about the power of good cataloging. Ginny Walter, for pointing out to me that I did not have to start my writing with chapter 1. Craig Russell, math teacher extraordinaire, for his many "technology tidbits" and enthusiasms. Greg Smith, for his über technical skills, his collegiality, and his enlightened view of the role of a system administrator. The teachers at Uni High, for their collaboration and for allowing me to play with their classes.

My sons Daniel and Simon, both now in their post-teen years, for sharing their hindsight (and present sight), putting up with my stories, and giving me their moral support.

My husband, Mitch, for reading every draft at least twice, helping me think through innumerable conceptual problems, supplying me with references and insights, and dancing with me at every available opportunity.

1

Teenagers
and the Library

T eenagers and libraries. These are two words that are not often used in the same sentence, least of all by teens. Teenagers have definite opinions about libraries (Meyers 1999). Libraries are not cool places. Only losers hang out in them. Their staff is unfriendly and unhelpful. Libraries do not have enough technology. Libraries need to provide better books and materials. Libraries have too many restrictive rules and fees. Libraries are more like morgues than like places you want to be.

How did we come to deserve such a bad rap? We pride ourselves on our collections, carefully assembled to support curricular and independent learning needs. We buy popular fiction, subscribe to trendy magazines, and organize activities to encourage reading and to support the social and emotional needs of our users. We make interlibrary loan services available and work with our counterparts in other types of libraries—school, public, and academic—to enlarge the information world for teens. Unfortunately, though, we have not always been completely successful in our delivery of these services.

Despite professional guides and standards and our good intentions, libraries do not have a great track record when it comes to welcoming teenagers. Mary Kay Chelton (1999) found that school librarians actually spend a relatively small proportion of their time on information service encounters. Instead, "service" often signifies rote activities—such as helping with equipment—that have nothing to do with real human interaction and can be performed by staff with less education and training. Most distressing, the substance of most student-library staff interactions is enforcement related, being "directed toward traffic control, compliance with the district-mandated pass system, and conformance with behavioral rules" (106). Chelton concludes that teens remember more about how they were treated in the library than they do about the specific outcome of the visit.

Teenagers have long been marginalized in the public library setting as well, relegated to a "problem patron" category all their own (Chelton 2001, 2002). Yes, teenagers arrive in hordes when school dismisses, appearing to use the library only as a place to socialize until dinnertime. During those few hours, many of them create havoc with the equipment and disturb "legitimate" library patrons. Chelton reminds us that adolescence is a distinct developmental stage of life, characterized by social learning. A teenager's "work" is to challenge authority, to find a balance between what one is told to do and what one wants to do, and above all, to learn how to be a communicator in order to build social relationships and feelings of belonging (Grinter and Palen 2002). Library staff, however, seem to expect learning in the library to be a solitary pursuit. Interactivity should occur only with library resources or staff. Chelton argues that this prevailing attitude "flies in the face of one of the most important maturation processes of adolescence, namely, social competence" (2002, 27).

Teenagers have personal as well as academic needs that ought to be met by library services. Up to 60 percent of a typical midsized public library's users are under the age of eighteen (Walter 2003). The teenagers among these young users are in the library to do homework and research, but also to check out CDs, to read magazines, and to see and be seen. Librarians do not need to compromise their professional standards or personal values to accommodate teenagers. Teens are better served by simply employing the same courtesies that librarians would use when working with adults. For example, Chelton (1999) witnessed school library staff asking students questions like "What do you need?" While there is nothing technically wrong with this question, as phrased, it rings out like a challenge. The emphasis is on the "you," on the inherent otherness of the new arrival. Chelton suggests simple adjustments in tone and language to indicate respect and caring, such as asking "Hello, how can I help?" The emphasis is then on the "I," the implication being that the institution and the staff exist to serve the new arrival. Besides alterations in verbal tone, there are nonverbal ways to indicate welcoming and to instill a sense of belonging. Libraries can create social spaces for teens. They can purchase overstuffed chairs as easily as straight-backed ones. The collection can be built to reflect teen interests.

Failure to follow through with appropriate service to teenagers is only part of the story. Even without the sting of insensitive or inadequate treatment, teens are still unlikely to want to spend much time in libraries. Loertscher and Woolls

(2002) ask some tough questions in their overview of the research on teenage users of libraries. What do we know about when and why teens use libraries? Do teens regard libraries as an essential service in their lives? Do teens feel that the library, even a "perfect" one, is important to them? Loertscher and Woolls speculate that the paucity of research on this topic is due to the fact that scholars already know what they would discover, what the library's ratings would be. "Even if we limited our questioning to 'things in school that help me succeed,' would the school or public library rank in the top five?" (31) The authors are doubtful.

Libraries are places that can easily induce feelings of inadequacy in adults as well as teenagers. One is *supposed to* know how to use libraries, *supposed to* hunger for the knowledge all those books represent. The teenagers who do not go to the library on a regular basis may avoid it because of the "supposed to" factor, as well as the hostile reception they have received in the past. Any efforts to make amends have met with less than outright success, in part because teens' primary experience with libraries is in the context of schooling, of information needs that are imposed by others.

THE IMPOSED QUERY

Melissa Gross (1999) has developed an intriguing line of research on the "imposed query," that is, information seeking that is externally imposed rather than self-generated. The imposed query, in and of itself, is not a bad thing. We often very much want to find the thing we have been asked to find. But for a young person, the imposed query is often linked with unhappy circumstances—homework, a difficult teacher, a weekend with no free time. And it follows that libraries are often associated with the unpleasantness of imposed queries. Libraries become places to look for information *other* people want you to find, not for information that you yourself find intrinsically compelling or valuable.

Interestingly, Gross found that younger children ask a preponderance of self-generated questions in the school library, but that older children (upper-level elementary) primarily ask imposed questions. Again, our good intentions as educators seem to go awry. If imposed queries rule the day, what has happened to the notion that true education begins with the curiosity of the learner? The importance of inquiry-based learning was first articulated by John Dewey (1902, 1915), and its value continues to be widely recognized and discussed (Stripling 2003; see also "The Inquiry Page" at http://inquiry.uiuc.edu). But in practice, we seem to be actually killing the instinct to satisfy natural curiosity in the library. Extrapolating from Gross's research, one can assume that the imposed query phenomenon continues to escalate through the teenage years. So even in the best, most teenager-friendly library, teens are bound to approach the library with caution, even attitude.

EVERYDAY LIFE INFORMATION SEEKING

What about the everyday "stuff" that people need to find out? The self-generated query? Contemporary researchers now study "everyday life information seeking" (ELIS), a relatively new branch of information studies (Savolainen 1995; Spink and Cole 2001). There is a difference in how people go about meeting everyday life information needs from how they approach information needs that are associated with occupational or school-related contexts.

> In occupational or school information seeking, the user is seeking information in a controlled environment with a definite end product that has some sort of paradigmatic quality to it. ELIS, on the other hand, is fluid, depending on the motivation, education, and other characteristics of the multitude of ordinary people seeking information for a multitude of aspects of everyday life. (Spink and Cole 2001, 301)

Can library information systems cope with the unpredictable demands of everyday life information needs? It is easy to make the case that there has always been a disconnect in how library users, teenagers included, have viewed "library" information as opposed to "real" information, the kind of information that is necessary to managing one's everyday life. For example, I think it is unlikely that my mother would call the library for help with a recipe, even though the library's shelves are stocked with cookbooks. She would call a friend first. And the typical teenager working on a car is much more inclined to seek information from a friend, a relative, or the local garage before checking the auto mechanics collection at the library.

It is true that the library is full of people using cookbooks and auto mechanics guides. The two information realms are not mutually exclusive. But they tend to be used in different ways. My mother might go to the library in advance of an event to browse cookbooks and get ideas for recipes. But in the heat of battle, when a vital ingredient is missing or the cake is not rising the way it should, other information resources may be more appropriate. For many sound reasons, teenagers and adults have always used and will continue to use informal, non-library information networks for immediate, everyday life information needs.

FORMAL VERSUS INFORMAL INFORMATION SYSTEMS

I have discussed two basic motivations for seeking information: the imposed query and everyday life information seeking. Such divergent needs require different types of information retrieval environments: formal systems and informal systems. Formal information systems are intended for the finite, definable scope of occupational and school information seeking. Library catalogs, databases, and their companions are formal information systems. By contrast, informal information systems are generally context-specific, varying widely in appearance and manifestation. The local beauty shop may host an informal information system, as does the bulletin board in the college student union.

Brenda Dervin (1976) identifies several false assumptions that information professionals hold about user information needs. One of these assumptions is that information is acquired only through formal information systems. In fact, people generally report that their use of formal systems is low. Even highly educated individuals rely heavily on interpersonal sources like friends and colleagues. Dervin disagrees with our professional habit of labeling this behavior a symptom of the "law of least effort" in the acquisition of information. Instead, she points to another faulty assumption—that "objective" information is the only *valuable* information. Users need information that is both objective (i.e., factual, datalike) as well as interpretive, contextual, and subjective. To satisfy both types of needs, we require both formal and informal information systems and services.

Formal Information Systems

Formal information systems are developed to be consulted and queried in purposeful ways, meaning that users must have some idea of what they need to know. This last phrase sounds facile, but anyone who has worked with teenagers (or other information seekers, for that matter) has learned that this knowledge of the destination cannot be assumed. Formal systems are designed in top-down fashion by experts who use highly defined rules for classification and retrieval. The rules may or may not be fully understood by users, but are the key to successful information retrieval. Users must take some responsibility to learn an information system's attributes, adapting their queries to match the system's functionality. Formal systems, though ordered and generally intended for universal access, are not perfect. Their boundaries and characteristics often elude users, who then have difficulty translating their information needs into forms that can be processed by the system.

We are surrounded by formal information-retrieval systems in modern society, not just in the library. The yellow pages of the telephone book are organized by topic and provide cross-references that guide users to system-defined categories.

Users must be able to navigate the alphabet, follow hierarchical subdivisions, and produce alternative terminology when cross-references are not adequately supplied. Hospital directories are fairly simple formal systems, typically listing doctors and departments by specialty, and possibly offering an alphabetical name index. Still, the consumer looking for an ear, nose, and throat specialist may need to know to consult the directory under "otolaryngology."

Informal Information Systems

Informal information-retrieval systems generally evolve from the bottom up rather than the top down, emerging directly from the community of users. The local barbershop clique forms over time, relying on the participants themselves to be information providers. In such cases, users do not *search* so much as they *share*. When consulting informal sources of information, users (wittingly or unwittingly) acquire auxiliary information. The teenager who visits a local mechanic for advice also discovers what the garage smells like and which tools the mechanic actually uses on the job. My mother, in consulting a friend, finds out how a finished dish should feel to the touch and what happens if one ingredient is substituted for another. Informal information seeking also encompasses habits of information consumption, such as reading a daily newspaper or having the radio playing while going about one's household chores.

In the informal environment, information often comes *to* the user rather than the other way around. When we open the daily paper or read the day's dose of weblogs, following various links embedded in the entries (and then hyperlinking in serendipitous ways from those), we are not so much looking for specific information as we are letting information come to us. We then filter this information through the perspective of our current needs and interests, some of which may not have even reached our consciousness. Finally, formal information systems can be used as informal systems. People search library catalogs, but they also browse the shelves and select materials they might not otherwise have thought to look for.

Teenagers: Formal or Informal?

Where do teenagers fit into this formal-informal information systems picture? Most research on adolescent information seeking has been applied to the imposed query environment, whether the object of that searching has been traditional formal information systems or newer, electronic systems (Neuman 2003). While it continues to be important to understand teens' information use in the context of formal learning, there is little research that describes teenagers' self-directed information needs (Walter 2003). We do not know much about what teens search for and why. It certainly appears that formal information systems are losing out with the teen audience. Teens generally use them only when required to, in the context of the imposed query. At the same time, it is not entirely apparent that teenagers differentiate clearly between informal and formal information environments.

Dresang (1999) opines that "researchers have not been accustomed to studying competent youth in *serious yet informal* information-seeking situations, largely because such situations have rarely existed" (1124). Her view is that we need a new paradigm for studying teenagers' productive informal information-seeking behavior in today's nonhierarchical, matrix-like information environment. While it seems self-evident that teenagers overwhelmingly favor informal systems, *how* they use those systems may be much more purposeful than has previously been understood.

THE LIBRARY VERSUS THE INTERNET

Owing to its association with formal school learning, the library is typically regarded as a land of formal information seeking. True, people go to the public library to find a good book to read, keep up with financial news, or use the copier machine. But when it comes to finding Information-with-a-capital-I for imposed query situations, the library is what comes to mind. However, the times are changing. For everyday life information needs, and increasingly for imposed query information needs, many people—adults, teenagers, and children—are going elsewhere. And where is that elsewhere? These days, elsewhere seems to be the Internet, which has become both a boon to library service and a source of competition.

Is the Internet part of the formal information world or the informal information world? People tend to think of the Internet as an informal information system, perhaps because intermediaries (e.g., the library and librarians) are not required, so individuals are in control of their own search processes. But the reality is more complex than that. The Internet is a multifaceted global information system made up of interconnected local, national, and international computer networks and their associated services. The World Wide Web ("the Web") is but one of those services, albeit the most ubiquitous one. When people refer to "the Internet," they often mean "the Web." The Web itself is home to formal and informal information systems, as will be discussed in the next chapter.

The Internet includes other important services that are not web-based in structure, such as file transfer, e-mail, and Usenet news, which are among the oldest services of the Internet and predate graphical interfaces. These services use different network protocols to transfer information from computer to computer. So, for example, instead of HTTP, or Hypertext Transfer Protocol, these services employ File Transfer Protocol (FTP), Simple Mail Transfer Protocol (SMTP), and Network News Transfer Protocol (NNTP). The distinctions are blurring; these services are all now accessible through web clients. But the point is that the Internet is actually a system of systems, each one having a different technical structure and functional application, which, in each case, gives it formal or informal information-retrieval attributes.

The Internet is generally an excellent vehicle for everyday life information seeking. Its content and access tools are fluid, ever-expanding, and infinitely variable. Inquirers can use the Internet to quickly find answers to highly specific, arcane, or personal questions. The library, on the other hand, has highly structured information systems, which make it seem plodding and inflexible. On the surface, the library primarily provides an information function while the Internet does many things. The Internet is both the end and the means, due to its nature as a system of systems. For example, the Internet has extraordinary value as a communications tool. E-mail, the "killer app" of the Internet, is its most-used online tool (Madden and Rainie 2003). Searching for information is the first runner-up to e-mail, with eight out of ten online Americans using the Internet to answer specific questions.

In the Internet environment, communication and information retrieval functions are increasingly indistinct. Students e-mail documents to themselves, taking notes in one window while reading source material in another, instant messaging all the while. Consider the plethora of "Ask an Expert" services that are available online, which personalize high-quality content using communication channels. There is no library counterpart except for chat reference service, which came along relatively late in online communication history.

The Internet is an open medium. It enables content producers as well as individuals to publish information without the services of intermediaries. No editors, publishers, vendors, or catalogers are required to vet the information, reshape it, or contextualize it. Clearly, the Internet has profoundly changed the shape of the information landscape. Users flock to it because of its multiple attributes and its one-stop-shopping reputation. In an imaginary popularity contest, the Internet would certainly beat out the library, even in cases when the Internet may not be the most appropriate destination. But the competition is an artificial one because, for many reasons that will be addressed in this book, the two choices are not truly opposing ones. At the same time, it cannot be denied that the Internet "side" is winning the teenage market. Let's take a look at how that battle is going.

Teenagers and the Internet

How do teenagers use the Internet as an information resource? The most prolific and reliable sources of information on this subject are the reports produced by the Pew Internet and American Life Project (http://www.pewinternet.org/). The report on teenage life online (Lenhart, Rainie, and Lewis 2001) reveals that 94 percent of online teens use the Internet to do research for school. Of the teens surveyed, 71 percent report relying mostly on the Internet for their most recent big school project, 24 percent rely mostly on the library, and 4 percent use both equally. Reasons cited for online use are the Internet's ease, speed, and accessibility. Teens also use the Internet for personal interests, from fashion and music news to more sensitive topics that call for privacy while searching. The Pew report on college students (Jones 2002) shows an even greater disparity between Internet and library use, with 73 percent using the Internet more than the library for research and only 9 percent reporting that they use the library more than the Internet. The Pew report on parents (Allen and Rainie 2002) reveals that in a quarter of the families who have Internet access, children have been the first to master its use, often becoming the family members who teach their parents the technology.

For the conclusions reached as well as the questions *not* investigated, the Pew project's various reports are potentially frustrating for librarians. For example, in the report on teenagers, the teens do not seem to have been asked *which* Internet resources they were using for school research. Were they perhaps sometimes using subscription databases, which are web-delivered resources provided by the library? Students seldom differentiate among Internet resources to such a fine degree, especially when access is transparent and they can connect remotely.

The Pew report on college students (Jones 2002) is more explicit than the report on teens about the use of specific resources. However, the report is potentially more damaging to librarian egos. The researchers found that though academic resources are offered online, most students either do not know how to find them or have not been shown how to. The students are much more likely to go to commercial search engines to type in their research queries, using library computers primarily for web surfing, checking e-mail, and instant messaging. The study notes that "college students seem to rely on information seeking habits formed prior to arriving at college" (13), a finding which has interesting implications for school library media specialists.

A False Choice

At first glance, it looks like libraries are losing on two fronts. We are losing our traditional customers, the ones who would come in to use the formal information systems for which we have been the gatekeepers. And we are losing, or lost long ago, those who are engaged in everyday life information seeking. In this book I try to present the case that the situation is not nearly so simplistic. We are not facing an either-the-library-or-the-Internet dichotomy, a future in which the choices either belong to the Luddites or the technonerds. The Internet is now *in* the library and the library is in the Internet. The card catalog, *Readers' Guide*, and their descendants have migrated to a web environment. Librarians have dumped their vertical files in favor of links on their web pages. Reference sources are available both online and in print form.

The art of searching for information is evolving as well. Most users have not really grasped the distinction between the *visible* Web (searchable by standard web search engines) and the *invisible* Web (resources that are hidden behind subscription databases or other secondary search interfaces). They are more likely to search the invisible Web while in the library, where licensing agreements are transparent and skilled staff are present to assist. At the same time, everyday life information seeking is becoming more purposeful now that the Internet has made a body of "published" everyday life information available and search engines have provided a means of searching it. The Pew reports have documented levels and types of searching activity—the what—but have not really plumbed the why and the how. It is up to information scientists to follow up. Some trends, though, are clear. For teenagers, the really essential difference between the notions of "Internet" (visible or invisible) and "library" is the Internet's unique ability to facilitate communication and connection to others. For teenagers, information is nothing without communication.

INFORMATION AND COMMUNICATION TECHNOLOGY (ICT)

If communication is so important, how does it fit in with "information," as libraries know and provide it? "Information" has a different meaning for information professionals than it has for information consumers, particularly teenagers. Dervin (1976) spoke of this difference in terms of the "functional units" of information systems. For the library, the functional unit might be a book or a document or a website. For the individual, the functional unit is generally a *communication* transaction, or, as Dervin puts it, "responses, instructions, reinforcements, solutions, answers, ideas, companionships, assistances wherever and however they may be found" (331). In other words, librarians conceptualize their services differently than their customers do. From the user perspective, communications properties are key to successful information-seeking experiences. Without them, information remains inert, devoid of usefulness.

Dervin developed this line of thought in the 1970s, long before the Internet as we know it was even imagined. But the functional units remain essentially the same today because they are made of the same building blocks: human knowledge and human communication. The difference now is the ubiquity of today's information technologies, which makes the lines between information and communication blur almost beyond distinction. It is becoming difficult, even artificial, to speak about one without the other. In response, a new term has emerged for talking about these issues—ICT, or information and communication technology—which will be defined in some detail in chapter 3.

How does ICT look in the lives of teenagers? Is there a difference between Dervin's 1970s model and today's highly connected world? In pre-Internet days, when students wanted to compare notes, work together on homework, or share secrets, they whispered together in the library, met at each others' houses after school, or called each other on the phone. They also passed notes in class, wrote letters to pen pals, and kept diaries. Teens used formal information systems, primarily in the library, for school-based research projects. In today's world, teenagers have much more technology at their disposal. They use both formal and informal information systems for school-based research, at the library and elsewhere. They communicate using landline and cell phones, handheld devices, and communications software. They send instant messages and e-mail, they maintain online diaries, and post to web boards and newsgroups.

With the availability of so much information and communication technology, these ought to be halcyon days in the library for teenagers. And yet, for a variety of reasons, libraries almost always have prohibitions against the use of technology for communication purposes. These are important times to remember Chelton's admonition that social interaction among teenagers is developmentally appropriate, even necessary, and has a place in the library. Information and communication technologies are ideally suited to facilitate that development, just as much as teen spaces and study rooms in libraries do.

Making It Happen

In the conclusion of their book *Teens and Libraries: Getting It Right*, Walter and Meyers (2003) make a number of promises to teens on behalf of public libraries. One of these promises is that librarians will be adult professionals in all dealings with teens. This pledge means that librarians will respect teens by doing good work, by giving directions and advice but not being rigid or prescriptive, by providing structure and boundaries that promote development, and by having high expectations of them. This promise also means that librarians will simply be themselves, and not try to measure up to some (possibly ridiculous-looking) coolness factor. Librarians do not have to be cool themselves to provide cool library services.

Another promise Walter and Meyers make is that librarians will work *with* teens, not *for* them. This pledge has to do with shaping services that teenagers can own, that are informed by their habits and needs, and that they have had a voice in creating. Adolescence is characterized by a need to feel one can influence the world. Libraries can give teens an important opportunity to make a difference, to contribute to their communities, and to engage in meaningful participation. And everyone wins. By bringing their verve and insight to the library, teenagers have the power to make it cool in ways that librarians simply cannot.

But first things first. Let's go back to the beginning and look at how libraries and their information systems affect teen users.

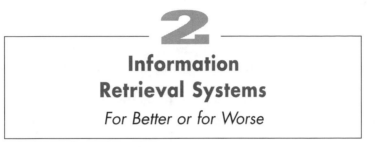

Information
Retrieval Systems

For Better or for Worse

A student of ours once ordered a book about the shipping tycoon Aristotle Onassis through interlibrary loan. I did not think this book was really what he wanted, since his history class was studying ancient Greece. When he came to pick it up, I asked him what his topic was. "Oh," he said, "it's Socrates," which he pronounced "So-crats." Restraining myself from smiling, I checked the cataloging-in-publication data on the back of the title page to see how a search on "Socrates" retrieved a book about Aristotle Onassis. It turns out that "Socrates" was Onassis's middle name (which may explain something about the kind of person he became). The combination of my student's lack of background knowledge and his propensity to use keyword searching was his undoing.

Libraries used to be less complicated places than they are now. At least, the options for finding information in them were more finite. We used three basic tools to unlock their treasures: the card catalog, a few periodical indexes, and the reference collection. A few others, such as the vertical file, a regional union catalog, other specialized indexes, and maybe a community resource file were also at hand but played less prominent roles. These were the bread-and-butter tools librarians used and taught teenagers to use. Reliable warhorses, they worked reasonably well for conventional school assignments—the animal reports, the term papers on the death penalty, the maps for geography lessons.

Libraries are now densely populated with a variety of formal and informal information-retrieval systems, which teenagers find both a help and a hindrance. In this chapter, I will take a look at how teenagers use a variety of information retrieval systems, how they select and evaluate the material they find, and how the interactive/communicative properties of information systems might affect teens' information-seeking experiences.

FORMAL INFORMATION-RETRIEVAL SYSTEMS

Organization Challenges

Formal information systems contribute to teenagers' not-always-positive attitudes toward libraries. Yet formal systems, both old and new, are also at the core of what has always defined libraries and made them work. Reconciling the disconnect between teenagers and formal information-retrieval systems is essential if libraries as institutions are to survive through the next century.

Library information-retrieval systems such as catalogs, periodical indexes, and other information databases may be the ultimate expression of formal information-retrieval systems. David Levy (2001) put it this way: "Because of the scope of their enterprise, libraries have been forced to develop highly systematic methods of organization—methods that could work relatively satisfactorily for huge numbers of works, and that could transcend the skills and knowledge of particular individuals" (123). In order to maintain these methods of organization, elaborate profession-wide decision-making structures have evolved to govern cataloging practices. A goodly portion of this governance is devoted to subject access, an especially problematic area of cataloging since it relies on the vagaries of human linguistic interpretation. The Cataloging and Classification Section (CCS) of the Association for Library Collections and Technical Services, itself a division of the American Library Association (ALA), is the home of many committees and task forces charged with establishing and maintaining subject cataloging standards. The CCS works with other ALA committees, with representatives from the Library of Congress (LC), and with the H. W. Wilson Company, which publishes the Sears List of Subject Headings.

Consider these examples of the care and consideration taken by various entities involved in the establishment of American cataloging practices. In 1999, the CCS Subject Analysis Committee's Task Force on Library of Congress Subject Heading Revisions Relating to the Poor People's Policy was charged to review and make recommendations on thirty-three proposals for new and revised Library of Congress subject headings that described poor people. This task force produced a forty-eight-page report detailing the extensive discussion the committee members held regarding bias in subject headings (Association for Library Collections and

Technical Services n.d.). On a more practical but no less complex level, in 2003 the Subcommittee on Subject Reference Structures in Automated Systems submitted a twenty-page report of "recommendations for providing access to, display of, navigation within and among, and modifications of existing practice regarding subject reference structures in automated systems" (Association for Library Collections and Technical Services 2003). It is important to note that these examples relate only to subject access in library catalogs. Similar intellectual effort is expended by a wide range of organizations, companies, and researchers in designing retrieval systems for other types of information repositories. Indexing and abstracting are disciplines in and of themselves. Clearly, no small amount of energy and focused intelligence has been devoted to refining and improving the formal information-retrieval systems we use.

Yet, with all the earnest effort these various initiatives and mechanisms represent, standard library information-retrieval systems are difficult for many people to use, particularly young people. Why is this? To be a successful searcher, and not just a lucky one, the user needs some understanding of the structure of a system before using it. The characteristics of formal information systems that seem to be especially tricky for users fall into three general categories:

Abstraction: A representation of the real thing

Vocabulary: Whose? And how much?

Classification: A book can only be shelved in one spot

ABSTRACTION: A REPRESENTATION OF THE REAL THING

Any catalog, database, or index is, by definition, an abstraction of the content it seeks to describe. A bibliographic system can be searched only by the tags that have been designated to represent its contents. The contents of an entire book are represented by three, perhaps four subject headings. A magazine article is much shorter than a book, yet receives the same degree of representation. The user must therefore determine the appropriate level of abstraction (or specificity) for a search. If my goal is to find a recipe for marble chocolate cake in a cookbook, my search term will have to be broader than "marble chocolate cake," probably something like "cake." Much as I would prefer to think otherwise, it is unlikely that someone has written an entire book on marble chocolate cake—which is what a successful search on that topic in a catalog would signify. Understanding how the formal information-retrieval system is structured, I will know that individual recipes in cookbooks are not assigned their own subject headings. On the other hand, I may have some luck searching on "marble chocolate cake" in a periodical database. This is an example of the mental shifting that must occur—the user has to consider the degree to which specific pieces of information are represented in information retrieval systems and how a subject might fit within a topical hierarchy.

To further confuse matters, formal systems now come in multiple flavors. In addition to the abstract bibliographic representation type, we have access to full-text systems and, more commonly, to hybrid systems in which both bibliographic and full-text information can be searched. Full-text searching means searching the real thing, not an abstraction or representation of it. But there are problems associated with full-text information retrieval. Here is what happened when I searched on the term "running" in a major periodical database of the hybrid type. The system defaults, as most do, to a keyword search, which encompasses the bibliographic record (title, author, subject headings, etc.) and the abstract. I retrieved 6,466 items using this default search, which varied from articles about people running for political office to articles about athletes running marathon races. My term generally popped up in the abstract field of these results, and less often in the subject field. When I restricted my search to the subject heading field, I retrieved 310 articles, all on the subject of running as a physical activity. When I chose the option of searching only the full text of the articles, I retrieved 107,525 hits. Searching the full text may be searching the real thing, but the price of high recall is pretty poor precision.

It can be difficult for users to fathom why their searches either work or do not work. Most formal information-retrieval systems cannot provide personalized feedback. Imagine a pop-up window in the catalog instructing me to "click here to see the results of your search, this time using 'cake' as a 'subject term search'"! Without search results differentiating between subject headings and keywords, decent results are often buried in the midst of other, not-as-relevant hits. Naive users often resort to improving their searches through trial and error, a process that reinforces the feeling that "library searching" is a hit-or-miss affair. The ability to search both bibliographic information and full text is a wonderful thing, but users still need to understand the underlying structure of a system in order to obtain meaningful search results.

VOCABULARY: WHOSE? AND HOW MUCH?

What do I look under? "Latinos" or "Hispanics"? "Movies" or "motion pictures"? "Chinese art" or "art, Chinese"? Controlled vocabulary is the tool that is used by formal information-retrieval systems to standardize terminology, ensuring consistency and stability throughout the system. Cataloging rules and conventions establish subject term structure, such as how subheadings are ordered. But even as these techniques solve problems, they also present difficulties for users. For the virtues of consistency and stability, we must accept a certain degree of inflexibility. Natural language gets translated into terms that can become awkward and, in some cases, archaic or offensive. The user must therefore be the more flexible partner in this relationship. If there is no cross-reference from "ear, nose, and throat" to "otolaryngology," the user must be prepared with an alternative terminology to test.

The structure of subject headings can be hard for non-librarians to fathom. A student looking for books about African Americans and their participation in the Civil War will need to use this subject heading: "United States -- History -- Civil War, 1861–1865 -- Participation, African American -- Juvenile literature." The two key concepts are buried at the third and fourth levels of the string of headings. Commas instead of double dashes are used in two of the subdivisions. Our student could conduct a keyword search on "Civil War" (and even add "African Americans"), but in a library of any size will retrieve far too many irrelevant hits.

Pauline Cochrane (1986), in her text on improving Library of Congress subject headings for use in automated catalogs, suggests that subdivision coding be permitted (i.e., subject subdivisions be coded individually) for greater flexibility in retrieval. In describing preliminary discussions held at the Library of Congress about how this task might be accomplished, she reports: "Since the logic behind the [subject heading] string's construction is lost on most catalog users and some catalogers, a worksheet was devised to guide the cataloger who would analyze a work and assign subject headings in parts or 'elements.' These parts would then be available for computer manipulation to construct headings for catalog cards and for computer-based catalogs, with varying display options" (62). Unfortunately, this proposal did not move beyond the discussion phase.

Cataloger Sanford Berman is perhaps the library field's most persistent (and sometimes controversial) voice for subject cataloging reform. In terms of cataloging for teenagers (1987), he identifies two major weaknesses in contemporary cataloging practice: the choice of vocabulary used for Library of Congress subject headings and the LC's stinginess in assigning headings. In his view, LC vocabulary is stilted and, at the time he was writing, rife with terms teens did not use. His examples include the LC's choices of "Adolescent boys" instead of "Teenage boys," "Teen-age marriage" (with the awkward hyphen) instead of "Teenage marriage," and "Youth" instead of "Teenagers." Many of his recommendations for changes have come to pass. The clinical term "Adolescence" is now reserved to describe books about child development. "Teenager" has finally become an official subject heading, though older records in many libraries' catalogs continue to bear the earlier terms. This duality, in which different materials on the same subject can be found under old as well as new terms, is another source of confusion for library users who are trying to make sense of the system.

Berman (1987) also views the sheer paucity of headings assigned to each record as being a huge problem for teenage library users. Fiction has only sporadically been assigned subject headings, which is a shame given the number of issue-oriented novels written for the teen audience. How would a teenager find a novel that features an anorexic protagonist if looking up "anorexia" yielded no fiction? For nonfiction, Berman criticizes the Library of Congress for assigning so few headings to each record. As an example, he uses the cataloging record for Elaine Landau's book *Different Drummer: Homosexuality in America* (1986), which was given the sole subject heading of "Homosexuality" by the Library of Congress. By contrast, the Hennepin County (Minn.) Public Library, Berman's home library at the time, supplied eight subject headings: "Homophobia -- United States," "Gay teenagers," "Gay teenagers -- Interviews," "Gay teenagers -- Family relationships," "Lesbian teenagers," "Lesbian teenagers -- Interviews," "Lesbian teenagers -- Family relationships," and "AIDS."

Berman (1984) also needles the Library of Congress for its humorlessness, which he saw as part of the general rigidity of the institution's modus operandi. The book *Should You Shut Your Eyes When You Kiss? Or, How to Survive "The Best Years of Your Life"* (Wallace 1983) is a sarcastic, tongue-in-cheek "survival guide" for teenagers. The following advice for navigating school cafeteria food is typical of the book's overall tone: "Go for food that was made somewhere else and brought in, sealed. Like milk, ice cream bars, potato chips. The next safest stuff is cold: sandwiches, coleslaw. Stay away from hot food except vegetables (but who wants to eat vegetables anyway?)" (23). The LC subject headings for this book are "Youth -- Life skills guides," "Students -- Life skills guides," and "Youth -- Family relationships." While the author most likely intended a serious message to seep through, the book is written in a wholly satiric manner. The Hennepin County Library's subject headings for this book included "Teenagers -- Life skills guides -- Parodies" and Teenagers -- Family relationships -- Humor."

Progress has been made since Berman wrote about subject cataloging for teenagers in 1987. "Gay teenagers" is now a Library of Congress subject heading. But change is slow. In the preface to the 1993 edition of his 1971 book *Prejudices and Antipathies: A Tract on the LC Subject Heads concerning People*, Berman is pleased to report that some of his original recommendations have become reality. However, he notes that it took thirteen years for the Library of Congress to finally abolish "Jewish question" and eighteen to get rid of "Yellow Peril." He laments the rate at which the Library of Congress addresses reform and societal change. Even when headings change, individual libraries may or may not be equipped to retrofit their catalogs to reflect the changes. Thus, some books will still be found under "Homosexuality" while others will be found under "Gay teenagers." To the user, how can this not seem like a conspiracy to make things more difficult than they need to be? And some headings never change. I know how much my students are confused, and sometimes even offended, by the subdivision "Juvenile literature." They do not think of themselves as "juveniles." (See exercise 2-1.)

I do not mean to single out the Library of Congress's subject cataloging practices as being particularly inadequate or uniquely odd. Most information retrieval systems that use a controlled vocabulary are guilty of similar idiosyncrasies. In my

---

EXERCISE 2-1

Sometimes there seems to be a certain level of absurdity, even surrealism, in many of the Library of Congress subject headings we see. Try this guessing game. Which of the following are (or have been) genuine Library of Congress subject headings? The answers are printed at the end of the exercise.

	YES	NO
Afro-American women in motion pictures	——	——
Booby traps	——	——
Cookery (Apples) -- Juvenile literature	——	——
Drive-by shootings	——	——
Education of princesses	——	——
Empty nesters	——	——
Freight-cars on truck trailers	——	——
Garbage can models of decision making	——	——
Internet addiction	——	——
Lesbian nuns	——	——
Milk as food	——	——
Poor teenagers -- United States -- History -- Twentieth century	——	——
Prostitutes' customers	——	——
Rednecks	——	——
Road rage	——	——
School shootings	——	——
Spin doctors	——	——
Virtual pets	——	——
Zorro television programs	——	——

Answer: If you answered yes to all, you win! All of these headings are or have been legitimate Library of Congress subject headings.

search for information on teenagers' information-seeking behaviors and their uses of catalogs in the H. W. Wilson database *Library Literature*, headings were few in number (one to three per article) and similarly broad. In some cases, the headings were so broad as to be almost meaningless: "Microcomputers -- Children's Use," "Internet -- School Libraries," "End-user Searching -- Case Studies." Who still uses the term "microcomputers"? The 700-odd hits I retrieved from this search were far from all being on the topic I was actually interested in.

It is probably more equitable to scrutinize the complexity of formal information retrieval by comparing the way a topic is treated across different systems. Budd (1996) conducted an interesting experiment with the literary criticism term "reader-response criticism," which has alternate terminology in the field and is used somewhat inconsistently. His study compared the results of a search on the heading in the Library of Congress database to the citations in a bibliography from a highly regarded book on the topic. There was little overlap, with only three of the titles from the bibliography turning up on the list of 245 titles retrieved from the Library of Congress search. Of those 245 titles, many were not in English and many others were practical treatments of the theory not addressed by the bibliography.

Budd found more overlap when comparing the bibliography to the *Modern Language Association Bibliography*'s search results, though more than half of the books retrieved in the *MLA Bibliography* search were still not included in the Library of Congress results. When that half of the books were checked in the LC catalog, along with the missing titles from the book bibliography, Budd found that LC subject headings other than "Reader-response criticism" were used. Most of those headings were anchored by the word "Literature" and were typically quite broad (e.g., "Literature -- History and criticism -- Theory, etc."). These vague headings would not be of much use to someone looking for books on reader-response criticism.

What conclusions can be drawn from this experiment? Because the coverage of the *MLA Bibliography* is literature, its headings are focused and faceted. Library of Congress headings, on the other hand, cover a world of knowledge and are selected by catalogers who are not subject specialists of the same order as those who do the indexing for specialized databases. Budd observes that the questionable benefits of large results sets generated by such broad terms as "Literature -- History and criticism" are not worth the loss in the precision and relevance of those results. He concludes that "perhaps it is unrealistic to expect a structured resource, like a library's catalog, to be equipped to impose order on all complex inquiries" (Budd 1996, 115). He recommends, as a partial solution, increasing the number of subject access points. The results of Budd's experiment make it easy to understand the importance of the informal "invisible college" used by scholars and academics. As Case (2002) notes, "all kinds of scientists and scholars satisfy much of their information needs through contact with their colleagues in the workplace and at conferences" (238), and not through the catalogs and databases provided by libraries.

CLASSIFICATION: A BOOK CAN ONLY BE SHELVED IN ONE SPOT

Finally, we have the problem of classification. A shelver emerged from our library's stacks one day in a state of extreme frustration. "Books on countries are in at least three different places!" she exclaimed. She was right, of course. Books on the history of a country are in one section and books on "description and travel" in that country are in another section. Books on the economy of the country, on women in the country, on the music or art or literature of the country—all are given different classification numbers, which disperses them throughout the collection. Even books on seemingly narrow topics can be found in multiple physical locations. Budd found that the books on reader-response criticism were scattered among several Library of Congress call number areas.

Yet we know that users, both novice and expert, browse the shelves as a means of finding the information they want. And librarians have long taught the principles of classification systems and have posted Dewey Decimal charts, in part to facilitate productive and serendipitous browsing. Once a user determines which call numbers are likely to yield success, those sections of the stacks become destinations. Yet, if it can be argued that there are not enough subject access points in a catalog, how can users be limited by a single classification designation?

Searching Challenges

So what does happen when young people interact with formal information-retrieval systems? As mentioned earlier, the user must be the more flexible partner in this relationship. Formal systems are what they are. They can be changed; but to maintain the integrity of the system, they are not designed to change rapidly. The real question is how the user adapts his or her behavior to the demands of formal systems. We know more than we used to about children's and teenagers' search experiences, although Walter (2003) points out that we still do not know much about their information needs. More research has probably been done on children's use of information systems than on teenagers' use of them. However, much of the research on children's use of online catalogs has relevance to the teenage (and maybe the adult) population.

The decade of the 1990s was a period of some rather intense research into children's use of library catalogs. It was important work, since research on this topic had previously focused primarily on adult users, and catalogs had always been designed with the adult user in mind. Moore and St. George (1991) found that children had trouble generating alternative search terms, and would give up their searches rather than try again with new terms. Solomon (1993, 1994) divided children's catalog search failures into three types: (1) idiosyncrasies of the software, (2) the characteristics of Library of Congress subject headings, and (3) the skills of the users. I find it telling that two out of these three types of failures are related to the structural characteristics of formal information-retrieval systems and only one type of failure has to do with users' skills.

SEARCHING LIBRARY CATALOGS

Solomon and others discovered access methods that were more suited to children's needs and abilities (Solomon 1993, 1994; Moore and St. George 1991; Raaijmakers and Schiffrin 1992). For example, children, even more so than adults, are better at recognition tasks than at recall tasks. They can often recognize what they need when presented with a list of choices, but are unable to produce information from memory, without a prompting context. This recognition factor is why most people typically perform better on multiple choice or matching tests than on fill-in-the-blank tests.

In the information retrieval environment, recognition skills mean that young users can identify terms they want from a list of terms, as well as select alternative terms they might not otherwise have thought of. But coming up with terms without such a list is a much more difficult task. Similarly, teens and adults would benefit from browse displays of precoordinated subject-heading strings, which show the true range and availability of topics in a way that keyword searching cannot replicate (Mann 2003). Children also do well with graphical displays of subject hierarchies because the hierarchies prompt recognition and can be populated with topics that are familiar to children (Walter and Borgman 1991; Borgman et al. 1995).

Hirsh (1999) found that students put much stock in the information provided in catalog notes fields in order to determine relevance. This is an important finding given how many catalog records do not contain data in that field. As Berman suggests, the more information a catalog record can provide, the better. Drabenstott and her colleagues (1999) studied children's and adults' understanding of subdivided Library of Congress subject headings and made some interesting observations as well. Their empirical research supported Cochrane's recommendation to break up long subdivided headings because the logic of the order is confusing to users and does not increase their understanding. They also suggested that heavy users of catalogs—children, adults, and reference librarians—be involved in the establishment of new subject headings and subdivisions. Finally, they recommended that the punctuation between subject heading elements be reexamined. Users simply do not understand the logic of the ordered, double-hyphen convention.

Much of the research described above, particularly that conducted by Paul Solomon and the Science Library Catalog group at UCLA (Walter and Borgman 1991; Borgman et al. 1995) was very influential in the development of the commercial product called Kid's Catalog (Busey and Doerr 1993). Kid's Catalog (now available from the Library Corporation, http://www.tlcdelivers.com) provides children with multiple modes of searching which meet the needs of different developmental levels. Users can search by keyword, explore a subject hierarchy of Dewey-inspired categories, or look through an alphabetical list of popular topic links. However, as important as the catalog research of the 1990s and the development of the Kid's Catalog were, this progress must be viewed in perspective. The focus group data from the Science Library Catalog research revealed something that most of us know but are reluctant to acknowledge. The library catalog—in either card or electronic form—was always a resource of last resort for these kids. Their first choice was to browse the shelves, their second choice was to ask for help, and their third and always last choice was to use a catalog.

SEARCHING OTHER SYSTEMS

Catalogs are not the only type of formal information-retrieval system that present difficulties for young users. Databases, indexes, and electronic reference tools all present similar challenges. The experienced library media specialists in Neuman's Delphi study (1995) concurred that "chief among students' problems in using electronic information resources are generating search terms, designing effective search strategies, and overcoming mismatches between personal ideas of how information is organized and how information is actually organized in databases" (297). In her summary of the research literature on this topic, Branch (2002) noted that "novice searchers lack the ability to form effective search plans and queries, cope with searching obstacles, [and] assess, refine and select results and synthesize data" (14). Most of the participants in Branch's study did not use advanced features, preferred using a single search strategy, and became frustrated when they did not get the results they expected.

Hirsh (1999) produced similar findings in her study of fifth-graders who were looking for information about famous athletes. These students became discouraged when their results did not match what they were expecting to see. They typically began with keyword searches, typing in the athlete's full name. When they encountered resources that were sensitive to name order, their searches were often unsuccessful. In general, they did not keep track of their search strategies and often were unable to reconstruct their searches. Some of the students in this study were unclear about the contents of the periodical database they used, thinking it indexed books rather than magazine articles. At the high school and college levels, we often see this misconception in reverse, with students assuming that the catalog doubles as a periodical index. In actuality, the catalog may provide access to the titles (i.e., the library's holdings) of periodicals but not (at least, not yet) to their contents. Both situations demonstrate that the ability to formulate viable search strategies is only part of the equation. Students also need to have good mental models of the structure of the resources they are searching.

AFFECTIVE FACTORS AND SEARCHING

How students *feel* about their task and about their own progress as they move through the search process influences their ability to be effective searchers. Branch and Hirsh both drew on the work of Kuhlthau, whose Information Search Process Model (Kuhlthau 1997, 2004) takes into account the critical role of the affective aspects of searching. The origin of the search task is also bound to have an impact on students' feelings about the task, as Melissa Gross learned in her imposed query research. Clearly, much of the research that young people do has been imposed by others, typically teachers in the context of schooling. This phenomenon may explain Walter's 2003 observation that we know very little about young people's own information needs. They never have a chance to express them!

Students' sense of ownership of a task will vary depending on the feelings and beliefs they have about their teachers and the level of understanding they have about the task. Gross also pointed out that "the query is in constant peril of mutation as it is passed along, transacted, and returned" (504). Parents frequently become involved in the research process, which results in a "double-imposed query" situation (and possibly familial strife). These factors, which are unrelated to the nature and structure of formal information-retrieval systems, nevertheless have a profound impact on how young people use those systems.

What to Do?

Even the founders of our modern cataloging and classification systems acknowledged that no system could possibly be perfect. In terms of subject access, Charles Cutter (1876) declared: "No catalogue can exhibit all possible connections of thought. Enough if it exhibit the most common, and give some clew [sic] for tracing the rarer ones. Those that claim perfection for any system show that they have no idea of the difficulties to be overcome" (541). Melvil Dewey (1876) held a similar view of classification schemes: "The impossibility of making a satisfactory classification of all knowledge as preserved in books, has been appreciated from the first, and nothing of the kind attempted. . . . Theoretically, the division of every subject into just nine head[s] is absurd" (625).

I would add to the words of these sages that not even a psychic cataloger can predict how a book will eventually be used or regarded, even in terms of something so seemingly straightforward as its subject. Early child-care manuals, etiquette guides, and legal handbooks are later used to study social history, yet their subject access typically remains fixed as originally assigned. Exceptions occur when collections are cataloged at later dates. The "Historic American Sheet Music" collection on the Library of Congress's American Memory website (http://memory.loc.gov/ammem/award97/ncdhtml/hasmhome.html) was cataloged as part of the digitization process by the holding library at Duke University. With the hindsight of late twentieth-century sensibilities, catalogers were able to develop a specialized thesaurus which contains terms like "Legacies of Racism and Discrimination -- Afro-Americans." This heading was used to describe 351 pieces of sheet music, including songs with titles like "Go to Sleep, My Little Pickaninny" and "An Educated Coon Is Best of All." Had these items been cataloged at the time of their publication, the subject headings would certainly not have included the term "racism."

If formal information-retrieval systems are so complex and counterintuitive, what can be done to improve them? That subject is fodder for another entire book; suffice to say, there are many folks working on the problem. Fourie (2002) advises a "socio-cognitive" approach to the teaching of indexing and abstracting. She urges library and information science educators to do more than merely teach students to follow rules and guidelines set by textbooks and standards. Information retrieval systems must be understood as belonging to particular discourse communities. Future indexers need to learn to work in a manner that is responsive to the subject vocabulary and information needs of the community they are indexing for.

INFORMAL INFORMATION-RETRIEVAL SYSTEMS

When discussing informal *systems* of information retrieval, the World Wide Web is the one environment worth a concentrated examination. Like the formal systems discussed already, the Web is intended for Searching-with-a-capital S. And like other formal systems, the mechanisms for searching both help and hinder users.

Organization Challenges

It is hard to talk about the Web in terms of its organization when it is, as a whole, not an organized system. The Web is home to a great unwashed marketplace of ideas, a 24/7 information asylum that is open to all. The self-published information it hosts is not—in its totality—selected by anyone, nor is it cataloged according to the Anglo-American Cataloguing Rules, warehoused in a single location, or archived. Any of it may be modified at any time. There are no principles that guide the structure of the Web's information retrieval tools, no Library of Congress catalogers, no American Library Association committees. To further confuse matters, the Web encompasses both formal and informal information-retrieval systems and resources. After all, the Web is where I consult the Library of Congress subject authority file and where I struggle with the subject headings in *Library Literature*. A large portion of what has become known as the "invisible Web" consists of the formal information-retrieval systems that reside on the Web—the proprietary databases and archives that are accessible only through their own search tools. But the visible Web is not well-represented by these search tools. So how do people find what they want?

For all practical purposes, web searching began with Yahoo, a subject directory service which employed human editors to index websites by topic within hierarchical categories. The web-searching field has since exploded. Search engines and subject directories abound, ungoverned by any centralized principle or authority. Furthermore, web search tools are generally commercial enterprises in competition with one another. They do not share their technical information or content, unless one search engine company buys out another. The depth and breadth of the coverage of various search tools are difficult to assess because their systems are not open to public scrutiny.

Search engine criteria for relevance determination vary widely, even changing over time. Machines instead of people do the selecting (crawling) and indexing (ranking algorithms). Since human judgment is generally not directly involved, relevance criteria include not only word matching but also other factors that can be computer-calculated, such as the "link-to" frequency from other sites. "Sponsored" links, paid for by advertisers, generally appear at the tops of results lists, and paid placements can appear (unidentified) throughout lists. Imagine online catalog results that display "sponsored" titles first, followed by the most popular as well as the most relevant titles. The popularity index may actually not be a bad idea, but ad-peppered catalogs are unpleasant to imagine.

Web search tools come in some basic types:

Search engines: Search tools that retrieve websites by sending out automated "crawlers" to roam the Web and index pages. Results are ordered according to formulas that weigh search term placement and occurrence, links to a site from other major sites, popularity, and other factors.

Metasearch engines: Search engines that search several other search engines at one time.

Subject directories: Search tools in which human editors categorize websites into hierarchical, nested subject categories. Some subject directories are highly selective and specialized.

Internet portals: Gateways to the Web that offer several services, one of which is web searching. Commercial portals tend to focus on shopping, travel, and business-oriented activities.

These days, most search tools do not fall into "pure" types and the field is in constant flux. A search engine may offer a subject directory service that is actually powered by an outside company. The reverse can also be true. For a time, Yahoo, originally a pure subject directory, used Google technology for its web-searching service. HotBot, once an individual search engine, is now a metasearch engine, querying several other engines besides its own (though these come and go). An interesting development in the subject directory world is Open Directory (http://www.dmoz.org), a community-produced search directory with annotated links that are contributed by innumerable users and organized by thousands of volunteer editors (B. Bruce 2003). Open Directory is an open source project, meaning its code can be shared and its structure and contents improved by the community. Individual users can import portions of it to a personal or school website, creating their own customizable index to the Web. Perhaps the greatest significance of this project is that now anyone can help index and organize the Web, in addition to contributing content. I am only half-joking by observing that Open Directory represents the democratization of cataloging.

The web-searching field changes so fast that it is difficult for the average user to keep up. Services such as Searchenginewatch.com and Searchengineshowdown.com are devoted to evaluating search engine performance, staying current on corporate buyouts in the sector, and reporting on cutting-edge technology and the other trends that can seem so dizzying to the rest of us.

Searching Challenges

Though web search tools seem easy to use, searching the Web effectively still requires some skill. The user must adapt his or her search strategies to fit the type of search tool that is used. Search engines are searched by keyword or phrase. Most search engines offer advanced features that enable users to focus their searches in a variety of ways, from specifying domain or file type to using Boolean operators. Subject directories are designed to be browsed, the user drilling down through hierarchical headings and viewing lists of related subtopics. However, most users tend to go straight for the search box, meaning they are actually using the search engines that general subject directories like Yahoo provide. The results pages include links to the subject categories, so the user gets the best of both worlds (without possibly realizing it).

In teaching my students the differences between search tool types, I advise them to use a search engine when they are looking for something extremely specific (e.g., the name of the drummer of a rock band) and to use a subject directory when they are just "looking around" (e.g., exploring types of rap and hip-hop music). The pure subject directories, especially those that are highly selective or specialized, can be trickier to search because they index only the equivalent of bibliographic information—not the full content of each website. The Librarians' Index to the Internet (http://www.lii.org), for example, can be explored through its subject hierarchy or users can type in search terms. But the terms are only matched against a bibliographic citation (with Library of Congress subject headings!) for each website plus a several-sentence description of the site. Users who expect search engine-like results are inevitably disappointed.

Web searching is the "easy" way to find information, according to most teenagers. The Internet has replaced the library as the primary tool for doing research for significant school projects, with 94 percent of online teens reporting that they use the Internet for this purpose (Lenhart, Rainie, and Lewis 2001). But how successful are these searches? Searching the Web has been likened to "visiting a shopping mall the size of Seattle: Innumerable types of information, in a large variety of containers and in many different locations, are all available in one place" (Fidel et al. 1999, 24). The students in a study conducted by Fidel and her colleagues (1999) had little knowledge of how the Web worked, who put information on "it," and who "ran" it. Most seemed to think the Web was some sort of central repository.

Still, the students in this study approached web searching in a predictable pattern. Their searching was very goal-oriented. If they did not find the information they needed fairly quickly, they would switch to a different topic for the assignment. In other words, the students were focused on the requirements of the assignment, not on their interest in the particular topic. Right in line with Gross's (1999) imposed query theory, students scanned websites for the information that would "fill in the blanks" of the assignment (28). Their searching was "swift and flexible" (29). If one site did not have what they wanted, they would move on to another site. When all else failed, they would just start over, using new terms.

All these behaviors are strikingly similar to the way we see teens search formal information-retrieval systems like catalogs and periodical databases.

Fidel and her colleagues suggest a number of enhancements to web search tools that would help students improve their searching. A number of these suggestions have come to pass since the time of their study. History lists serve as navigation "landmarks," search engines like Google offer alternate spelling suggestions, and advanced search pages feature multiple ways of refining a search. But it is not clear that novice searchers actually take advantage of these aids. The evidence indicates otherwise. Hirsh reports that the fifth-grade students in her study "did not make use of advanced search features, and did not use navigation features" (1999, 1278). Furthermore, these kids did not keep track of URLs and had to keep re-creating good searches.

Even after experiencing difficulties in finding appropriate information, the students in the Fidel study viewed web searching as being more convenient than looking for information in the library. After all, one only has to type in terms to get instant information, as opposed to the tedium of looking in the catalog, writing down the call number, then having to "go through all the aisles, look for the book. . . . It's boring!" (27). Students in this study enjoyed searching the Web, saying they would use it for their next assignment. Several students volunteered the opinion that the Web was more fun when they were not looking for a specific thing, when they just wanted to surf.

SELECTION AND EVALUATION CRITERIA

Formal Systems

How do young people typically select and evaluate information retrieved from formal systems? Selection and evaluation criteria are influenced by the nature of the information need, the cognitive ability, and the developmental level of the student. Is the reading level of the material appropriate for me or is it too advanced or technical? Do I need a lot of information or a little? Do I need a popular treatment or a scholarly one? Students are taught the differences between magazines and journals. They are told not to use the health information they find in *Glamour* magazine if an assignment calls for rigorous biological research literature. At the most sophisticated level, students are taught to spot political perspective and determine point of view.

What is the reality of student searching? Librarians express much angst over students' tendency to simply snatch up the first several citations of a results list, barely checking for relevance let alone suitability or authority. We watch students take home a pile of books, then return all but one or two the next day. We wince as they print out articles we know they do not need, discarding the "extra" paper in fairly short order. When students display these behaviors, they may simply be following principles of least effort as they rush through an uninteresting assignment. Or perhaps these tactics may be their way of responding to the information overload caused by the volume of information they encounter. As people find more and more information, and have decreasing amounts of time to process it, they resort to simpler and less reliable rules for making selections (Case 2002). A "collect-then-discard" strategy may be the most effective and practical way for young people to master the problem of information overload.

The findings of Hirsh's study of fifth-graders' relevance criteria are intriguing. Besides relying heavily on the notes field in the bibliographic record, they used visual and organizational cues to assess the utility of a source. These elements include the book cover, its title, the table of contents, and the back-of-the-book index. They determined relevance primarily by examining the text for topicality, relying heavily on the assignment's requirements (the imposed query). But students also placed a high value on personal interest attributes, the novelty of the information (i.e., that it was new to them), and the material's potential for peer interest (since they were required to make a presentation to their classmates). As students moved through an assignment, they were less concerned about topicality in general, and became more focused on filling in specific gaps in their research. During the selection process, they did not consider authoritativeness, accuracy, or truthfulness of information when assessing materials for relevance. For the most part, they appeared to trust the information they found, regardless of source, and did not even think to question its validity.

Hirsh makes a distinction in students' selection and evaluation behaviors based on the nature of their task. She argues that even imposed query tasks can be personally interesting to students. Motivated information seekers will spend more time poring over lists of results and evaluating the information they retrieve. She posits that because the students in her study found their topic (famous athletes) to be interesting, their search behavior differed from that of students in other studies. Hirsh found that most of the students in her study expressed ownership of their topics and demonstrated care in their examination of bibliographic data and the visual and organizational attributes of sources. Her findings undermine our notion of the stereotypical student researcher who rushes through a task to get it out of the way as quickly as possible.

How has the evaluation of information retrieved from the formal library "canon" of books, periodicals, and reference tools changed with the advent of the Internet? I believe that some of our previous care in teaching evaluation skills has fallen away. Instead, we have had to turn our attention to the vast wash of the Internet, focusing on teaching students to first look for information that is merely credible. "Merely credible" is not much to ask for, but it must be addressed. We know with absolute certainty that students will encounter websites developed by such "authorities" as conspiracy theorists and people with axes to grind. Nevertheless, the "old" selection and evaluation issues have not disappeared. There is still a difference between *Newsweek* and the *Bulletin of the Atomic Scientists*, between the local community newspaper and the *New York Times*. But with the bar set so low to accommodate the Internet, perhaps teaching about those distinctions is endangered.

The Web

One of the biggest complaints teachers and librarians have about students and the Internet is kids' apparent lack of discrimination among the Internet's many resources. Educators' fears are supported by the research, which Hirsh (1999) summarizes by noting that "students, from elementary school to high school, do little evaluating of the accuracy of the information they find on the Internet; they tend to assume that the information they find is true and valid" (1267). In the Fidel study (1999), the students (and, interestingly enough, their teacher) evaluated sites according to whether or not the information they needed for the assignment was present. In other words, they used the assignment as an evaluation filter rather than using criteria like the authority of the website creator or the reliability of the information.

Agosto (2002) looked at Simon's model of decision making in her study of adolescent girls and their evaluation of websites. She focused on Simon's concept of "satisficing" (1979), or how people tend to use practical boundaries to simplify their decision making. Because it is not realistic to weigh all outcomes and fully explore every possibility, people generally choose to settle for something that is acceptable, even though it might not be optimal. I would call this the "good enough" principle. The practical boundaries that Agosto's teenage girls identified were time constraints, information overload, and physical constraints. Her analysis echoes Case's summary of the effects of information overload (2002). Agosto is more optimistic than those of us who assume that teenagers just make choices based on the principle of least effort. The "good enough" principle assumes a process anchored in reasoned criteria, whereas the "principle of least effort" assumes no process at all.

Agosto also studied the effect of these girls' personal preferences on their decision making, seeing these as reflective of the affective piece of Kuhlthau's process model (2004). Agosto found that personal preference played a large role in the girls' evaluation of individual sites, which they judged based on graphical and multimedia elements as well as their level of personal interest in the subject. She notes that "many of the participants dismissed the Women of NASA site solely based on its background color" (26). I wonder if these girls would have been so quick to reject a site if it was one they identified for their own needs rather than one they were looking at for an outside researcher.

We do not really need research to tell us that teenagers are not always careful or reasoned evaluators of information they find on the Web. And this discussion has not even touched on how teens make choices in chat rooms, how they evaluate the credibility of newsgroup postings, and what they do with queries from unknown e-mail or instant messaging correspondents. But to play the devil's advocate, I would suggest that as individual teenagers become full participants on the Internet scene—the more they create their own websites and participate in online communities—the more sophisticated their perspectives become. By jumping in as real players, it is inevitable that they improve their understanding of the Internet's structure and content. We already know that many teens are skeptical of the information they see on websites because, having developed websites themselves, they know how easy it is to publish online (Lenhart, Rainie, and Lewis 2001). In the act of contributing their own content, their comprehension of the nature of other online content deepens.

INTERACTIVE AND COMMUNICATIVE FACTORS

Does it make sense to think about formal information systems in terms of their communicative and interactive properties? Or are we talking about a read-only, one-way environment? Yes, one can write letters to the editor of a newspaper (online or in print), an activity which is both interactive and communicative. But are we stretching to come up with this one example? Perhaps we are using definitions of "communication" and "interactivity" that are too narrow. Information systems and resources themselves may not be "interactive," but the searching and selecting processes certainly are.

Hirsh found that the fifth-grade students in her study shared resources as they searched and did not hesitate to ask their school librarian for help. One student reported that a friend identified a source for him while this friend was doing his own searching. When asked about his search strategy, the student concluded that "I kind of found it on accident" (1270). Yet why should his find be considered accidental? This type of collaboration is also a strategy, one which can be encouraged and enabled. These students, their teacher, and their librarian were exploiting the attributes of the library-as-place, a physical space in which information sharing is natural.

Fidel and her colleagues (1999) found that when students used the Web, "searching was both a social and an academic event. They [the students] conversed with one another while searching, asking questions and giving advice" (28). These teenagers were also proactive about asking for help from the librarian and the teacher. I think it can be argued that communication is just as important a tool in information searching as is the understanding of information systems. We already know that social communication takes place in libraries. There are undoubtedly connections between social communication and the information sharing that occurs. Communication bridges the gap between formal and informal information systems. People find ways to make information systems, whether formal or informal, work for them when they have information needs. The challenge for us is to remove roadblocks and enable the naturally occurring communication and information-seeking processes to work.

Information Technology Meets Communication Technology

What happens when digital information technologies and communication technologies come together? They become more than the sum of their parts. In merged form they have come to be called information and communication technologies, or ICTs—environments in which people use communication technology to access information, manipulate it, transform it, and exchange it. In his foreword to *Literacy in the Information Age*, Allan Luke places the communication role at center stage: "Digital information technologies are communications technologies, new modalities and media of human communications, nothing more and nothing less" (2003, x). By any definition, ICTs are social information spaces. They are designed as much for the reciprocal *sharing* of information as they are for seeking and disseminating information. "Seeking" implies going to sources outside one's immediate social system. Sharing involves exchanging information both inside and outside your own social group and signifies that you have as much to offer as you are likely to receive from others. ICTs can be bona fide communities with unique social norms and customs, just like other human communities. Finally, ICTs take on many forms, having evolved organically in response to a wide range of user needs.

Some ICT tools, such as instant messaging and e-mail, were originally designed for communication purposes. But users have turned them into information tools as well, making them full-blown ICTs. People insert web links into their messages, send pictures to one another, and share other types of information. As with so many tools of technology, users have changed the designers' original intentions simply by adapting the tools to their everyday habits and needs. Product developers have responded by adding features to enable these behaviors. In this fashion, technologies and their associated uses evolve over time.

The "millennial generation" (youths from the ages of thirteen to twenty-four) is the first to spend more time on the Internet than watching television (Harris Interactive 2003). It is no surprise that teenagers are major consumers of ICTs. Teenagers seem to be experts at merging information-seeking and information-sharing activities. The tools of ICTs fit naturally into their lifestyles and have come to represent their culture. Millennials are enthusiastic fans of instant messaging software, with 74 percent of online teenagers using it as opposed to 44 percent of their adult counterparts (Lenhart, Rainie, and Lewis 2001). "A typical IM session for a teenager lasts more than half an hour, involves three or more buddies, and often includes friends from outside her community" (3).

Teenagers use ICTs for maintaining friendships and for establishing new ones. Evidence of this phenomenon is all around us. Several years ago, a group of students at my school began a collaborative blog which consisted primarily of the typical banter, gossip, and party planning one would expect. When these students graduated, however, the blog took on a new life. It became a way for them to keep up with one another from a distance and to organize reunions during college breaks, as well as a forum for topical debate and discussion. I am convinced that their friendships remain stronger than they would have been without the blog.

Teenagers' academic lives also incorporate ICTs. The Pew report on "The Internet and Education" (Lenhart, Simon, and Graziano 2001) documented the role of communication technologies as homework helpers. Forty-one percent of online teens reported that they used instant messaging and e-mail to contact teachers or friends about schoolwork. These teens collaborated on projects and problems, received clarification about assignments from their teachers, and sent files to one another. My son told me of being instant-messaged a paper from a friend who asked him to proofread it. Web-based homework help sites have proliferated, ranging from online reincarnations of Cliff Notes-type sites to interactive "Ask an Expert" services. High school students are now often assigned to develop websites instead of term papers, to check their teachers' web pages for course updates, and to turn in homework online.

College students are "early adopters and heavy users" of the Internet, having grown up with computers (Jones 2002, 2). This generation leads the nation in interactive online activities like downloading music, sharing files, and instant messaging. Livejournal.com, an online personal journaling service, gets 20 percent of its traffic from college personal computers (Rainie, Kalehoff, and Hess 2002). College students' communication habits are not restricted to leisure. "For most college students the Internet is a functional tool, one that has greatly changed the way they interact with others and with information as they go about their studies" (Jones 2002, 2). Web-supported coursework has become a fact of college life (Jones 2002). Course websites contain assignments and provide links to pertinent resources. College students are required to e-mail other students, subscribe to electronic discussion lists, and complete coursework online.

ORGANIZATION OF ICTS

What are some of these information and communication technologies? What is their value as information resources? For purposes of the present discussion, I have categorized the various services somewhat arbitrarily based on type of activity and patterns of communication. My intention is to focus on those services that have the greatest influence on teenage life online. Therefore, I do not discuss every possible ICT that currently exists and I spend more time describing some ICTs than others. All are Internet services, though not all use the Hypertext Transfer Protocol (HTTP) communication protocol of the Web. Most, as exemplified by those described in this chapter, have the characteristics of informal information systems. Finally, I have left the mention of a couple of services, such as online gaming, for further exploration in chapter 4. Moreover, technology is a swiftly moving target. The individual tools and applications I describe here will change. Future services will no doubt aggregate their functions in different ways and otherwise morph into forms I cannot begin to imagine.

Given these caveats, here are the categories I will delineate for this particular moment in ICT history:

Personal ICT environments: Personal web pages, blogs, and online diaries

Collaborative ICT environments: Usenet and message boards, electronic discussion lists, chat rooms, peer-to-peer file sharing

One-to-one ICT environments: E-mail, instant messaging

Already, these categories are not tremendously distinct from one another. There are collaborative blogs, websites that include message boards, blogs with comment areas, and so on. One of the most interesting mergers of information and communication spaces can be seen in shared hypermedia (SHY) systems, which integrate computer-mediated communication tools with web browsing (Riva 2002). Different users who are simultaneously browsing the same website can "see" each other, communicate, and share information. The participants have the web page in common and may be part of a larger community of people who share interests. SHY systems and other innovations will continue to alter the ICT landscape.

PERSONAL ICT ENVIRONMENTS

Personal Web Pages

Personal websites have been part of the Web since it began and are the ultimate expression of the Web's role as a democratizing agent in modern society. Personal web pages have become even more prevalent since the widespread availability of free website-hosting services and graphical website-design software. Obviously, the value of personal websites as information sources is widely divergent. Personal websites vary from the site of a fourth-grader who posts a page about her dog to the site of a serious meteorology enthusiast whose local storm data is as reliable as comparable data from the National Weather Service. Finding information in personal websites is the job of search engines. Site creators improve the chances of search engines retrieving their sites by employing coding techniques valued by search engine crawlers and by (somehow) making sure their sites are linked to from other highly trafficked sites.

Blogs and Online Diaries

A weblog, or blog, is a personal website that consists of brief entries generally written by one person, with the newest entry posted at the top of the page. What makes a blog different from any other personal web page? Blog analyst Rebecca Blood (2002) says that the defining characteristic of the blog is its format. New entries are *always* placed at the top and the site is updated frequently. The page typically has a sidebar with a list of links to like-minded blogs and to sites the blogger has especially selected. The difference between blogs and online journals or diaries is often negligible, though the blogger tends to strive more for communication, while the web diarist is more focused on self-understanding. Many blogs are characterized by short journal entries focusing on the writer's daily life. Other blogs are characterized by longer entries with more topical content, usually about issues going on in the larger world. The writer's personal commentary takes center stage, but nearly all bloggers link to the source material they discuss. As editorialists, bloggers provide a context for their sources.

Blood notes that "a good weblog on any subject provides a combination of relevance, intelligent juxtaposition, and serendipity" (12). Blogs attract readers with similar interests and points of view and build followings based on trust in the taste, judgment, and presentation of the creator. "When a weblogger and his readers share a point of view, a weblog constantly points its readers to items they didn't know they wanted to see" (13). Almost like our psychic cataloger. A blogger named Ryo Chijiiwa has attempted to facilitate this serendipity by creating a search service called BlogMatcher (http://blogmatcher.com), which helps users find like-minded blogs. When the user enters the URL of a blog he or she likes, BlogMatcher searches for other blogs that link to the same sites, operating on the assumption that common linking signifies common interests.

How do teenagers use blogs? Little research has been done on this to date, but quick scans through the many thousands of blogs that exist show that the ones created by teens are primarily of the diary type. Teen blogs also frequently feature interactive elements like polls, where readers cast votes on issues ranging from the hottest new music act to the latest crisis in the Middle East. Xanga.com is a good example of a blog-hosting service that seems to attract a large teenage following. Many entries are written in the slang styles that characterize online communication among teenagers. The following is an adaptation of an entry I read recently that uses an interesting mix of hip-hop slang and other abbreviation styles that are common in the online environment:

> hey. sup? as for me juss chillin n playin cards wit my bud alyssa. 2day i did some of my assignment for AP Biology and went and chilled over at my best friend jenifers hizzouse. we chilled, talked, and watched men n black. hehe. i watched dat movie before. shur is funny.
>
> driving school was cool. imma drive on monday @ 400! w00t!!! lolz. im excited then im scurrd. but i guess it will be a good experience for me. umma . . . ahh . . . well im chattin wit 2 of my buddies so umm im out. buhbyes peace~ -smilez-

The content of this entry is typical in the way it integrates many facets of the writer's life and work habits. She relates events from her school life and her social life, expresses fears about learning to drive, all while instant messaging with two friends.

If one is to judge solely by the blogs they link to, teens read and follow blogs that are like their own. Teens also migrate to the blog services their friends use. They report "having a Xanga" or "starting a livejournal," rather than using the generic "weblog" or "blog." In some cases, they take advantage of services that are target-marketed to teens. Teen Open Diary (http://www.teenopendiary.com) hosts diary-type blogs, but it also sponsors "diary circles," where teens cross-post their comments to shared boards on topics like movies and poetry. The entries on these circles link back to the posters' diaries. Registered users are also allowed to post comments to other members' diary entries. This practice is similar to "traditional" blog structure, but certainly constitutes a new spin on the personal diary concept.

It is important to note that teen blog aficionados do not always restrict their writing or reading exclusively to diary-style blogs. Teen bloggers can be quite serious in their writing, using the forum as an outlet for creative writing, political musings, or other earnest pursuits. There are many mainstream blogs that appeal to teen viewers, such as those created by celebrities or authors. For example, the writer Neil Gaiman maintains an online journal (http://www.neilgaiman.com/journal/journal.asp) in which he answers questions from readers, teens among them.

Blogs are not designed for targeted, deliberate searching. They are meant to be followed, integrated into one's daily online activity and routine. They meet information needs in the way that personal magazine and newspaper subscriptions do. To go back and find specific information in them can take some doing. Bookmarking or linking to specific information in a blog is tricky because individual entries shift from their position as current postings to archived postings, where they shift yet again as archives restructure themselves. Bloggers can embed "permalinks" with each entry, which allows others to link to that specific entry no matter where it resides on the blog. It can be even more problematic to try to find an entry in a blog that has come up in the results list of a general web search engine. The link from the search engine typically takes you to the current page of the blog and you can spend fruitless hours digging through the archives, trying to find the one entry you want.

Not very many individual blogs have search functions, though some of the big blog-hosting sites do. Registered Xanga members can search its blogs by keyword. Open Diary (http://www.opendiary.com) has an index by age and place. Blogdex (http://blogdex.net) is a project of the MIT Media Laboratory, which monitors the diffusion of information and ideas through blogs. Bloggers register their sites, which are then tracked by links. A keyword search of Blogdex turns up a list of linked-to websites. Each site in the list is "back-linked" to the blogs that originally linked to it. The user can find websites of interest as well as like-minded blogs.

Another way blogs can extend their reach is through syndication. Using RSS (Rich Site Summary), an application of XML (Extensible Markup Language), bloggers insert coding that packages the content as a list of data elements (e.g., date, heading, summary, entry, location—not so different from author, title, subject, and call number!). RSS content-aggregation software is used to query RSS-enabled blogs (or websites, for that matter) and display updated articles the user has not yet seen. In this way, the user knows when favorite blogs have been updated and can read the headers of new entries without having to check them individually. Syndication is not as difficult as it sounds. Most blogging software now accommodates the coding and all the user needs to do to activate it is check a box. Content aggregators can be downloaded as stand-alone software or accessed on the Web, such as the blog monitor Technorati (http://www.technorati.com). Besides searching syndicated blogs by keyword, Technorati users can search by URL to find out who is linking to whom.

As search functionality is added to the blog environment, it will be interesting to see if teenagers take advantage of it. We do not know much about teenagers' interest in searching blogs. Do they ever try to find something specific, or are they sticking with the core functions of writing, reading, linking, and commenting?

COLLABORATIVE ICT ENVIRONMENTS

Some key features distinguish collaborative ICT environments from one another. First, membership is either open to all or else limited to a defined set of participants. Second, contributions may appear online immediately or may have to be screened first by a moderator, who checks for appropriateness according to a predetermined set of criteria. Message-blocking criteria can include such factors as spam (unwanted commercial e-mail), obscenity, defamation of character, or content that is inappropriate to the topic of the shared environment. Third, collaborative environments are distinguished by mode and timing of message delivery. Information either flows to the user, as in e-mail, or the user goes to the information, as with web-based discussion groups. Conversations that take place over time, such as in electronic discussion lists or e-mail, are asynchronous. Conversations that occur during real time are synchronous, such as in chat room and instant messaging environments.

Usenet and Message Boards

Usenet news and electronic message boards are asynchronous group-discussion environments. Usenet, one of the oldest services of the Internet, is an internationally distributed, decentralized bulletin-board system and a world unto itself:

> Messages are clustered into newsgroups and are propagated around the world, server to server. . . . Usenet has been used for hundreds of purposes: schools set up private newsgroups so students can communicate between classes, and developers share strategies for programming. There are newsgroups dedicated to every conceivable purpose, and each actively discusses a wide variety of topics. (Fisher 2003, 11)

Usenet news is what used to give the Internet an especially bad reputation, with its notorious alt.sex groups. But Usenet has a long history as a serious communication and information-sharing tool for computer scientists and other professionals. Old-timers access the discussions using text-based software on UNIX systems, others prefer specialized graphical software clients, and now a big portion of the database can be accessed with a web browser at Google Groups (http://www.groups.google.com). These days, habitual Usenet consumers tend to be geeks, teen or otherwise. More mainstream users are likely to access Usenet through Google Groups, an easy way for non-geeks to use the service on a more occasional basis. Google purchased the Usenet archives from Dejanews, a now-defunct web-based archiving agent of Usenet discussions as well as a platform for reading and posting messages. It is likely that many of the people who use Google Groups do not even realize they are accessing the venerable Usenet, which predates the graphical Web by about ten years.

Usenet messages do not last forever. Local servers expunge them to make room for new messages, which number in the hundreds of thousands each day. Those who use dedicated newsreader software can only access these recent messages. Google Groups now maintains archives of most newsgroups, except for those that are not distributed beyond local servers. How does someone find newsgroup postings on specific topics? Until Dejanews came along, searching Usenet postings was not really possible. With its successor, Google Groups, users can now search for highly specific information. For example, fans of the television show *Friends* can easily look for discussions of the prom video episode by typing in three keywords: "friends," "prom," and "video." But contributors to Usenet should be cautious—the angry flames posted to soc.politics (or alt.tasteless.jokes or rec.nude, and so on) live on in the Google Groups archive even after they have been purged from local servers. The Usenet messages of John Walker Lindh, the "American Taliban," were later used to trace his descent into extremism.

Message boards are virtual topical bulletin boards, which can be found on countless websites. These boards are spaces where readers post questions, opinions, and other commentary. Message boards for teenagers abound. Studentcenter .org is an example of a service that hosts message boards (called forums), as well as blogs, chats, and diaries. The message boards are organized by topic, covering everything from fashion to GLBT (gay, lesbian, bisexual, transgender) issues. Nonprofit advocacy sites as well as commercial sites feature message boards. Teens can discuss their cancer treatment or the latest book by the science fiction writer Orson Scott Card. Message boards are not aggregated by any central server, linked by a common communication protocol, or organized under a common hierarchy as Usenet newsgroups are. So there is no good way to locate message boards unless one already knows the URL or can find them through a general web search. Their content can only be searched collectively through standard search engines. Retrieval odds are not good unless a searcher is able to target the query with other qualifying terms or parameters. Since message boards typically reside on individual websites, archiving practices are determined by individual website owners.

Message boards and Usenet newsgroups both feature a "threaded discussion" structure in which postings and their responses are nested so readers can follow the sequence, or thread, of a conversation. Participants can post follow-up messages to existing threads or post new messages that will initiate new threads of conversation. (See figure 3-1.) Participants can also respond directly to individual

Sep 15, 2005	How many shadow books coming?	kzbyn@hotmail.com
Aug 2, 2005	Ender's Game: the movie!!	Beanman
Aug 2, 2005	Re: Ender's Game: the movie!!	amblixer
Aug 3, 2005	Re: Ender's Game: the movie!!	Ebony W
Aug 4, 2005	Re: Ender's Game: the movie!!	Norm Thompson
Aug 4, 2005	Re: Ender's Game: the movie!!	Ebony W
Aug 4, 2005	Re: Ender's Game: the movie!!	Beanman
Jul 31, 2005	I know whut ur up to	nospam.net
Jul 28, 2005	Just discovered OSC	Charley B
Jul 28, 2005	Re: Just discovered OSC	amblixer
Aug 5, 2005	Re: Just discovered OSC	Tony Smith
Aug 5, 2005	Re: re: Just discovered OSC	hunnypie
Aug 5, 2005	Re: re: Just discovered OSC	Tony Smith
Jun 3, 2005	What order to read Ender series?	Tiff
Jun 3, 2005	Re: What order to read Ender series?	Ebony W
Jun 4, 2005	Re: What order to read Ender series?	Mystery man
Jun 4, 2005	Re: re: What order to read Ender	Tiff
Jun 4, 2005	Re: re: What order to read Ender	Mystery man
Jun 5, 2005	Re: re: What order to read Ender	kzbell
May 29, 2005	Anyone else heard about this?	Thecolonel
Jun 1, 2005	Re: Anyone else heard about this?	Mary Sue
May 15, 2005	My new Ender's Game site!!	Beanman

FIGURE 3-1

Example of a threading structure adapted from alt.books.orson-s-card, where participants discuss books written by Orson Scott Card.

posters by using e-mail. This option is employed when conversation ceases to become valuable to the group as a whole, but remains cogent for the primary participants. For example, someone may post a request to a collector's newsgroup for a specific item. Those who have the item to sell or trade will communicate directly with the poster through e-mail because these transactions will not be of interest to the community at large. When message boards and newsgroups are moderated, the tone and character of the discourse may change. Off-topic postings, spam, and offensive content are less likely to appear, but conversation will be more restrained than it otherwise would be.

The discourse style of most Usenet groups indicates that the "regulars" follow the threaded discussions on a consistent basis. As members of virtual communities, they have a vested interest in keeping up. Lueg (2003) suggests that traditional newsgroup inhabitants would be pleased to have information-filtering tools that search not only for topically relevant postings (as Google Groups does) but also for interesting or worthwhile discussion threads. Standard search tools can accomplish the former, but not the latter. In other words, Google Groups can match words and links, but it cannot detect rants and frivolous postings. Therefore, it's my guess that *habitual* newsgroup participants, teenage or otherwise, use Google Groups largely to identify newsgroups they might be interested in following, and only occasionally do they consult it to find specific information.

Perhaps it is primarily interlopers who use Google Groups to search for specific information. I will use myself as a case example, by confessing that I have used the search function to answer gardening questions. By typing in "cilantro" and "bolting" I can read postings, mostly from the rec.gardens, rec.gardens.edible, and rec.food.cooking newsgroups, that tell me that everyone's cilantro "bolts" (goes to seed) in the heat, not just mine. Yet I have never posted anything to those groups myself, nor do I follow them on a regular basis. Whether I am typical of Google Groups lurkers, I do not know. But without the searching functionality, the information I find valuable in Usenet would be lost to me.

Electronic Discussion Lists

Electronic discussion lists are another asynchronous form of communication. Users must subscribe in order to participate, and messages are delivered by e-mail directly to their mailboxes. By their nature, electronic discussion lists are more private than message board systems, and their communities can be small and quite selective. Some make their archives publicly available and searchable, such as LM_NET, the electronic discussion list for school library media specialists (http://www.eduref.org/lm_net/archive). Teenagers are probably less likely to

participate in electronic discussion lists than they are to use other types of collaborative online forums, which have more to offer them in terms of accessibility and
topicality.

Chat Rooms

Chat rooms are synchronous communication spaces. If Usenet gave the Internet
a bad name for its salacious content, chat has given the Internet a bad name for
the admission of pedophiles and other unsavory characters to its spaces. Both
stereotypes have a basis in fact but, like most stereotypes, just tell part of the story.
Chat spaces are often organized around specific agendas or purposes, such as the
chat room components of online distance-education courses. People go to chat
rooms to accomplish a task, discuss a topic of mutual interest, or just to hang out.
But the role of chat is generally centered on communication rather than on information, and so the focus is on the relationship rather than the task. In some cases,
the participants all know one another. In more public chat spaces, users do not
know each other and have no way of determining if their fellow chatters are who
they say they are. Probably for this reason, the days of high interest in joining public chat rooms with unknown others is waning (Harris Interactive 2003).

Conversations held in chat rooms are typically neither captured nor archived,
so their content cannot be searched later. There are notable exceptions, such as
the chat room conversations held by students in distance-education classes, which
can be searched later by students who missed class or by teachers who wish to
check on student participation levels. But in general, chat room conversations are
fleeting, like ordinary face-to-face group conversation, but without even the
impression of people's faces and voices.

Peer-to-Peer File Sharing

Peer-to-peer (also called P2P) file sharing is a mode of information exchange in
which computer users with the same networking software can access files on one
another's hard drives, without the use of a central server. Users designate which
files they will share, which makes them available for keyword searching.
Searching is handled by the software client, which sees other neighboring computers that are online and use the same client. Some computers are designated as
nodes, meaning they do the searching and then match computers that have the
desired file to the requestor's computer. The requestor then selects among these,
basing the choice on such factors as the connection speed of the host computer.
Searches are not global. If a desired file cannot be found one day, the user can try

again the next day and hope to be connected to a different node. Peer-to-peer sharing provides an excellent environment for collaborative work, and has included such prestigious scientific efforts as the Human Genome Project. Unfortunately, peer-to-peer sharing has earned most of its media attention for the illegal exchange of copyrighted media and software, and for the exchange of pornography.

Young people have become major consumers of peer-to-peer networks. College students lead other users in file sharing of all kinds, with 44 percent reporting sharing files from their own computers as opposed to 26 percent of the overall population of Internet users (Jones 2002). P2P users do not need fancy search skills, usually just the name of a song, an artist, a movie, or a piece of software they want. In a significant way, searching for something on a file-sharing network is similar to searching by title or author in a library catalog. These are all known-item searches. Unlike subject searches, known-item searches are simpler to execute since the terminology is typically easier to determine. However, file-sharing systems cannot yet be searched for "songs about cars" or "movies that have cats in leading roles." Do users understand that they are not searching a global system? I think most understand that if other users' computers are not online, they cannot share files with them. But I am not sure they understand that their searches are confined to the computers a node happens to be connected to at a given moment, or even that they can only search other computers that use the same networking software.

ONE-TO-ONE ICT ENVIRONMENTS

E-Mail

E-mail, an asynchronous form of communication, was one of the early drivers of the Internet. Its roots date back to the late 1960s with the development of ARPANET (H. Bruce 2002). Messages are sent from one computer to another computer, from one designated point to another designated point or points. In other words, e-mail messages are not broadcast to the world at large, to be picked up by recipients. A single message can be sent to multiple recipients, but the sender determines who the recipients are. E-mail has grown beyond its text-only beginnings. Graphical and web-based software allow users to embed links and graphics and to easily send file attachments. Because e-mail resides on individual computers and servers, it is not searchable in the same way that postings to message boards and newsgroups are. Individuals can generally search their own saved e-mail records, but not those of others. E-mail is the most private form of online communication, yet it plays a pivotal role in information exchange.

Instant Messaging

Instant messaging (IM) is a synchronous form of communication, with users typing back and forth to one another while both are online. Though conversations typically occur between just two people, users often have more than one conversation going at a time, with several windows open simultaneously. Most IM software includes chat service, in which multiple people can participate in the same conversation. Advances in technology include audio and video transmission, application sharing, and remote assistance, in which one user can see and manipulate the other's computer (Riva 2002). Unless a user deliberately logs an IM conversation, its contents disappear when the participants close their windows or log out. Still, users can send links, images, and other content to one another. IM is an ephemeral medium by nature, and the contents of unsaved conversations cannot be searched or retrieved later.

While instant messaging does not incorporate information searching per se, it does allow the placement of information "bread crumbs." Teens sort their buddy lists into a hierarchy that tells them, in order of importance, who is currently available. Away messages are often used as announcement centers. "I'll be at the mall all afternoon." "celly: 256-4212." Friends know they can check each other's IM settings to get useful, timely information without ever picking up the phone. Instant messenger profiles, as well as away messages, can be bloglike, containing a description of the author's state of mind, bits of poetry, quotes from saved IM conversations, or links to his or her personal web page.

These few paragraphs hardly capture the importance of these transient blurbs in teenage life. If a snapshot could be taken of all the teenagers who are online at a single moment, the vast majority would most likely be engaged in instant messaging conversations, some active, some dormant. Even more than e-mail, messaging technology is the "killer app" for teenagers, the epicenter of their online world.

What are the consequences of all this interconnectedness? Is teenage culture truly changing or are ICTs just new ways of accomplishing the same old things? In part 2 of this book, I will take an in-depth look at the consequences, both intended and unintended, of ICTs in teenage life and some of their ramifications for our society at large.

4

The Fallout

Intended and Unintended Consequences

T oday's ICT tools have lofty origins. The Internet itself began as a military research endeavor called ARPANET. Its purpose was to provide the U.S. military's research and development community with a secure and survivable means of communication. As a bonus, scientists would be able to use the technology to share data sets and research findings. The Internet still serves these purposes, but it has also absorbed countless other roles that were never envisioned by its original designers. Scientific researchers tend to conceive of their labors in terms of serious and important purposes. But the people who actually use the tools find ways to employ them that were never imagined in the laboratory. An interesting example of this is closed captioning for television, which was developed for deaf viewers. Its biggest implementation is in noisy bars, allowing patrons of those establishments to keep up with the game despite the din.

Consumers, including teenagers, have managed similar end runs with other ICT tools, transforming many advanced technologies into tools of social connection. Smart product developers observe the old adage—first watch where the people walk before laying the sidewalks. And teenagers are happy to demonstrate; they are consummate trend drivers, particularly when it comes to information and communication technologies. Marketing executives have learned that where teenagers go, the business world will follow (Foroohar 2003; Harris Interactive 2003). So a cycle begins. Designs are modified, new products are created, and campaigns are launched, all in response to the vagaries of the modern teenage mind.

It is interesting to observe the factors that drive the media choices of teenagers. Teens are dependent upon market factors (what is actually available), economics (i.e., parent purchasing power and willingness), and family dynamics (protecting family time, sharing the media). Simple logistics also play a part. Some teens, as well as adults, favor cell-phone text messaging because they do not always have access to a computer, while their cell phones are readily available. Teenagers are also motivated by what is happening within their peer group. If most people in the group use one type of technology, the others need to use the same type. There comes a tipping point when a specific technology wins the allegiance of the cohort. New members must conform if they want to belong.

Media choice is also heavily influenced by the user's goals. For example, magazines are an initial destination for current information on trends, fashions, and celebrities. In turn, magazines help direct a more focused online searching experience (Harris Interactive 2003). Grinter and Palen (2002) found that teenagers favor e-mail for formal activities, such as communicating with teachers and submitting college applications. It is ironic that most adults, including system designers, continue to think of e-mail as a vehicle of informal communication. Now, however, it is the medium of choice when the user needs to be able to edit, spell-check, and produce a more polished product. And all e-mail is not equal. One of my students told me that having an e-mail address from school "looks so much better than something off of yahoo or hotmail, makes you look a little more serious . . . or so I think."

In contrast, teenagers choose instant messaging for spontaneous one-on-one conversations or for group chats with friends they know in real life. And if they want to speak casually with people they do not know, they go to public chat rooms or other more open chat environments. These chat spaces are typically organized around defined topics that provide a link for participants who otherwise have no common ground with which to initiate conversations. Organized public chat rooms are treated as destinations, as goals in and of themselves. Instant messaging and e-mail are processes, means to an end.

THE DECLINE OF CIVIL DISCOURSE

Each time a new communication technology comes along, two extremes inevitably emerge. First are those who immediately jump on the bandwagon, purchasing unreliable beta-level products and wondering where everyone else is. Then there are those who cling to their old tools, wringing their hands over the impending loss of civilized communication, even of all civilization. We hear perennial concerns about the deterioration of social skills, the loss of intimacy and depth in communication, and the erosion of genuine human connection. Where educators and pundits once worried about the loss of face-to-face contact as telephone use increased, they now mourn the lost art of letter writing as e-mail use has grown. Others argue that e-mail is merely the successor to pen and paper, and that letter writing is now more robust than ever. Online correspondence is also a strange mixture of the private and the public. It is immediate, often impulsive, yet it can be planned and meticulously crafted. It can scroll off a screen into the ether or it can be saved and shared later, and not always by its creator.

New technologies *do* change patterns of language and written communication. Some changes are welcome, some are not, and some are just odd. After a period of use, we often forget their origins and they become business as usual. Naysayers rightly point to the preponderance of poor spelling and slipshod grammar in electronic communication. The immediacy of the medium and its perceived informality (at least in the minds of adults) certainly can contribute to a lack of attention to detail. But, as teenagers have realized, spell-checking and other editing tools are changing both perceptions and habits. And now, cell-phone text messaging (SMS, or short message service) makes the most primitive e-mail communication look eloquent. Between the per-character pricing structure and the minimalist writing palette, the writer is forced to be cryptic. But with improvements in technology—features as simple as hot keys (e.g., single letters that make complete words)—even this medium is bound to become more expressive. (See figure 4-1.)

In some cases, habits *should* change as a result of technology, but do not. The invention of the typewriter brought a do-it-yourself form of professional printing

FIGURE 4-1

For some teens, *any* technology is preferable to no technology at all.

into the business office environment and the home. Work-arounds were developed to compensate for the typesetting tricks that typewriters could not manage, and some of these oddly persist in an era of desktop publishing and word processing. For example, writers still commonly insert double spaces between sentences, which had to be done on typewriters to create adequate visual separation. But unlike monospaced typescript, letters produced by word processors are proportional and the extra space is not needed (Williams 1990). The Modern Language Association's style manual (Gibaldi 2003) still prescribes underlining titles instead of using italics, a holdover from the days of single-font manual typewriters.

The list goes on. Many commonly used abbreviations began life as a means of saving scarce space on the printed page. Their use became codified and they persevere in a digital world which does not require their space-saving attributes. Depending on the discipline and the format, bibliographic citations are still littered with abbreviations for journal titles, state names, and other terms (e.g., "Univ." for "University" and "Pr." for "Press"). Scientific styles still mandate using authors' initials instead of full first names, much to the dismay of interlibrary loan librarians.

Something Lost, Something Gained

Does change always signify decline? Or does change sometimes just mean change? While new technology takes away some things, it also gives back others. In the virtual environment, we lose visual cues, changes in tone of voice, and other subtle nuances that are clear in face-to-face interaction. But the virtual setting brings along its own cues and conventions. Participants are often more direct with one another, more candid, and so more "honest" than they would be otherwise. Contacts may be more frequent and spontaneous, if only because they are easier to initiate. There is simply less inertia to overcome, less start-up time. Everyone is infected by this ease, not just teenagers. Using e-mail and instant messaging, I have kept up with my far-flung middle-aged cousins as well as my teenaged nieces. One no longer needs a "reason" to make the contact or, as my nieces would say, it's just not such a big hairy deal any more. Online communication has great potential for increasing intimacy and closeness in human relationships.

I tire of the two-camp dichotomy—the split between those who condemn ICTs outright and those who regard them as the great modern panacea. Such positions are neither helpful nor illuminating. Technology makes communication and other aspects of modern life *different*. Yes, some things are better and, yes, some things are worse, but mostly things are different. Only future historians will be able to assess the impact of the accommodations, the attitude changes, and the behavioral shifts we have made. In the meantime, I subscribe to the perspective articulated by Nardi and O'Day (1999), who tell us to situate information (and communication) technology within ecologies of human activity. If a healthy, diverse system of users and functions is present, then we can be assured of a productive and beneficial outcome.

We do not need a crystal ball or the insight of a future historian to know some things about what ICTs mean in the life of a teenager. Today's ICTs provide teenagers with remarkable tools for personal and social development. Teenagers look to ICTs to help them accomplish two key, age-old functions of adolescence: personal identity formulation and connection to others. These two functions can seem mutually exclusive or, at the least, contradictory. Even as teens strive to be different, to be unique and independent, they want to belong, to be one in a group of many. When I sent an e-mail message to the students at my school asking them questions about their use of ICTs, I was showered with fascinating testaments that all pointed to these basic motivators and their inherent conflicts.

It is important to note that the students' comments (many of which are reproduced here) and my accompanying interpretations refer to specific tools and technologies, which are destined to be superseded or exchanged with other technologies. They are used here primarily for illustration. No matter what the present or future form of the technologies, they tell the same story—about the need teenagers have to find a sense of identity and community and how they do so through the use of ICTs.

IDENTITY

Adolescence is a crucial transition period from childhood to adulthood. It is during this time that we separate ourselves from our parents and find out who we are without them. This exploration of personal, independent identity is the most pressing developmental factor of a teen's life. There is much about the online world that allows for this exploration and experimentation. Teens who are fortunate enough to be "connected" have been quick to exploit these avenues. When they meet one another, they exchange e-mail addresses, instant-message screen names, and blog addresses. All are symbols of identity and status, and all are windows into the inner lives of each person.

Even "simple" IM profiles and away messages are used for so much more than what their supposed functions indicate. They are laden with pieces of self; they are used to share political viewpoints, original poetry, and links to websites of personal importance. They are also used to entertain and amuse. Icons and avatars reflect moods of the moment, alter egos, and current idols. Profiles are rarely used to merely describe one's demographics ("I'm a girl, I'm fifteen years old, I live in Peoria"). Instead, profiles are creative outlets, literary devices for recording what one feels and thinks. They are also used to solicit sympathy or express solidarity with others. One student told me:

> hmmmm, as for profiles. for me and a lot of people it's just a form of self expression i'd say. just to get whatever off your mind. or as you mentioned to show people weird links or something. song lyrics lots of time. or just weird stuff you find online that you paste the text out of. most of the time it's something i write though, just like whats on my mind. . . . sometimes just random stuff like "AGGGGGGHH HOMEWORK!" or countdowns till school ends.

Me, Myself, and I: Blogging

In creating blogs, teens make public the very private experience of adolescence. They publish their thoughts in the hope that people will read them and comment, yet are mortified at the very thought of such an eventuality. They like knowing that they can let it all out and are willing to risk others' judgment for the therapeutic benefits of making online confessions. They also get to display their wit and uniqueness in a way that everyday life does not allow. When people respond in supportive or appreciative ways, blog authors experience welcome validation. A teen who was interviewed by *New York Times* reporter Emily Nussbaum (2004) declared that he would go to a new friend's LiveJournal (a blogging service) before calling, e-mailing, or instant messaging the person because he felt an online diary was the best way to really find out about someone else. He could do this unobtrusively, without directly engaging the other person. Telling others about your blog is also a way to let them know about you without going through all that awkward introductory business.

As described in chapter 3, teenagers' blogs are typically of the online diary type. Though most include links to references, teens are much more interested in writing about their personal concerns and moods. One of my students, an especially reflective young man, had this to say about blogs:

> Blogs are indescribably useful :) I've had my blog for a little more than a year now (I started it December of my junior year, last year) and have used it primarily as self-expression space. Often this means that I whine a lot on my blog. Other times it means that I just get to comment on whatever is passing through my head—I think I did a string of "current events" posts like that last February or March.
>
> I think that at the high school level this is actually what most people use their blogs for: This is about me and my life and my friends and I'll say whatever I

please. You could easily interpret this as an extension of the "adolescent rebellion" phase. But I've seen a few blogs which have been running social or political commentary, or blogs that are operated as part of a project (someone, for example, blogged from Africa about a social effort that he was making there).

To summarize a bit, blogging is an extremely good form of personal journalism. It promotes free thinking and speech, it allows people to express themselves, and it allows people to get their message out across the whole globe without those silly constraints about intrusive advertising or web space. What people *do* with that power of journalism depends on who they are. But blogs are definitely a large part of our future.

The interactive nature of blogging is enormously attractive to teens. Old-fashioned private diaries lack that seductive component, the opportunity for attention and support from others. Friends pepper one another's blog entries with cheerful responses and encouragement, commenting on new design features and commiserating over strict parents and rocky relationships. Sometimes it is not the content that is so intrinsically valuable on a blog, but the feedback. One boy told me that "I'm not too interested in just reading them for my entertainment . . . it's just more like someone says 'hey read my blog' and I'll be like 'sure' and read it." Reading one another's blogs is a mark of friendship and loyalty. Teens also spend innumerable hours playing with fonts, colors, and other design features of their blogs. I know of one girl who changes her icon at least weekly. Blogs are teens' personal palette, a means of self-expression that costs little or nothing to maintain other than their own time.

Polls and questionnaires are popular features on blogs. Some just have links to the websites that actually contain the polls. Blog authors then report their "scores"—which star they would most likely go out with, what animal they are most like, etc.—on their own blogs. Some polls are devised by individual bloggers and may be very specific to a group of friends. Names are listed and questions asked. Who is the first on the list most likely to lose his or her virginity? What (name of music group) song are you? Some polls are just open-ended questions, generally philosophical. Will cold fusion ever be possible? What is your view of the afterlife? These exercises help cement the group identity as well as helping members to find their place in a bigger scheme of things, and understand more about themselves and others.

Rebecca Blood (2002, 163) observes that "a weblog is a bully pulpit" and argues for using the platform for the greater good. Rather than surrounding oneself with like-minded thinkers, replaying the familiar points of view and becoming insulated, she admonishes her audience of adult bloggers to instead use their forums to ask hard questions that would illuminate the news instead. Although few teen bloggers seem to maintain politically oriented or topical blogs, they do use blogs to craft careful reflections on their personal experiences. Blogging helps them develop observation skills and a meta-awareness they wouldn't otherwise have.

I like the phrase "personal journalism" in the way my student used it. It seems to cover the span of personal ramblings and gossip, interspersed with more "goal-oriented" content. Some teen blogs do have more of an agenda than the daily log of doings and random observations. I ran across one that is a joint effort of three teen artists who use the forum to display their work and get feedback from readers. The blog itself is a daily expression of the frustrations of being an artist (artist's block, distractions of homework and chores, problems with an aspect of the current work, etc.). Entries link to images of the actual artwork, with comments from readers appearing below the images.

In Control

ICTs afford an independence to teenagers that is otherwise difficult for them to achieve. Their school day is highly structured, leaving little time for socializing. Life outside of school can also be heavily scheduled with work, sports, lessons, family obligations, and other activities. ICTs can give teenagers control over the discretionary time they do have.

> It's not like watching television, Millennials [twenty-first-century teens] explain, where you have to wait for the weather to come on. And it's not like the radio where play lists are dictated to them. With the 'Net, it's their schedule, their music, and their friends, essentially when they want it. (Harris Interactive 2003, 19)

Messaging technologies are especially useful in this regard. Both IM and SMS can be used outside times that teenagers are normally permitted to be together, such as late at night, and messaging technologies are, for the most part, unobtrusive. Unlike a ringing telephone, instant messages do not disturb the family dinner. Cell-phone text messaging makes no sound in class. SMS is also useful for the teenager who is stuck somewhere, usually with parents. One student told me that she sends her boyfriend text messages from the car during family trips. The technology gives her the wherewithal to maintain what control she can over the private part of her life.

Keeping Parents at Bay

A major focus of adolescence is separating from one's parents and establishing an identity apart from them. Online communication provides a convenient door to an outside world over which parents have only limited control. Because teens tend to be the technology experts in their homes, deceiving parents can be remarkably easy. Teens know how to erase cache files on web browsers, track their parents' online presence and mask their own, turn off telltale sounds, sidestep filtering software, and hide their activities by closing windows and sprinkling their online conversations with coded language. Instant messaging functions below the radar in most homes. It can be used covertly, especially if the sound is turned off and the teen does not share the computer with others in the home. Even when it is used openly, teens typically try not to draw too much attention to IM within the family circle. It is their private space within a public world.

For all these reasons and more, parents often find that the Internet is a flash point of conflict with their children. They worry about the questionable content that can be accessed online, who their children are "meeting," and what other unsavory activities their sons and daughters might be engaged in. In some respects, parents' worst fears are true. Ordinarily mild-mannered teenagers swear like sailors online. They let the world know that their parents truly are stupid and clueless. They share intimate details of their lives, including what they have done that they have been expressly forbidden to do. They even seem to think of the oh-so-public Internet as a private place simply because their parents are not there. From the teenage perspective, the Internet is a gateway to independence. From the parental perspective, the Internet is a morass of unknowns over which they have no control.

Having It All

This is an exciting time to be growing up, a time full of options for enriching one's personal life. And teens want to take advantage of all of them. So rather than make choices, they have become habitual multitaskers. A teen may be searching the Web for a school project in one window, instant messaging with friends in other windows, and checking e-mail in yet another window. Grinter and Palen (2002) found that three primary activities characterize teenage instant-messaging communications—socializing, event planning, and schoolwork collaboration—all of which may occur during the course of a single IM conversation. And outside of the conversation, the participants are simultaneously carrying on with unrelated activities—talking to family members, sorting laundry, eating, listening to music.

Many teenagers are adept "serial multitaskers," moving from one cluster of activities to the next. As soon as they get home from school, they launch instant messaging software, check their e-mail, and eat a snack. While updating their own blogs, they read their friends' blogs and post comments to them. They instant message one another about their blogs and paste bits of their IM conversations into their blogs. They download music, listen to Internet radio, and create music playlists. At night they keep up this pace, in addition to interacting with family members and doing their homework. No single activity receives their undivided attention. Is this a generation adapted to overstimulation? Can teens really do so many things at once? Maybe not well, but certainly with less anxiety than adults. They have learned to develop highly effective compensatory strategies. For example, IM discourse is distinguished by its real-time, yet more-sequential-than-synchronous nature. Conversations "hiccup" as responses often come two or three comments below their direct antecedents. When I asked students about this, they were untroubled. One student wrote:

> hiccup conversations, as you call them, are extremely common but not a big deal. its difficult for me to think of any really absurd or funny ones because i just dont think of them that way. the receiver always gets it in the context of three lines ago or whatever instead of processing it as current, so it seems to make sense, at least to me.

Still, life can get very interesting when teenagers participate in multiple IM conversations. Keeping windows straight is a challenge, not to mention following the topic and tenor of each conversation. Making a mistake can have grave social consequences. If teens who are engaged in a group chat hold side conversations with some of the participants, a misplaced snide comment is difficult to explain. Several students indicated to me that their use of group chats on IM has declined because it is simply too confusing, even for them. One girl wrote:

> i dont do it very often because then its like extreme hiccup messaging. i never know whats going on. and if you leave for like one minute you will be completely lost in the conversation. especially if youre in a chat of like five people and two of those people are having their own conversation and then the other three are off on some tangent.

Getting There without Going Anywhere

Teenagers typically lack control over where they can go and how and when they can do it. If they are not too young to drive, they must share the family car. They generally have to negotiate their time away from home. ICTs allow teens another kind of mobility, one in which family rules and physical distances are irrelevant. Teens use technology to stay in touch with one another when they cannot physically be together. As an added bonus, keeping in touch with friends who are far away is just as easy as keeping in touch with someone who lives a block away. We are looking at a generation that does not understand the significance that long-distance calling had to previous generations. My mother still has to keep herself from watching the clock during long-distance calls. Today's teenager sees no difference between calling someone across the street and calling someone who is across the country. Virtual mobility also gives teens opportunities to communicate with people they do not know in real life, no matter what the location of the various parties.

ICTs are, of course, also used to facilitate face-to-face meetings. A friend of mine remarked that 90 percent of his kids' cell phone conversations with friends are about establishing where each person is. "I'm at the mall." "Hey, me too!" "Where?" "Lower level, food court." "OK, stay there, I'm coming down." And so on. Cell phones make it even easier for teens not to plan activities in advance, much to the consternation of their parents, who often feel blindsided by sudden turns of events. Though parents often get family cell-phone plans for security purposes, teenagers quickly begin to use them to strengthen personal communities outside of their families.

COMMUNITY

As much as teens want to be special, different, and unique, they also want to fit in. They need to belong, to feel they are part of something larger than themselves, and to know that they matter to the group. On one side of the equation, we have the adolescent's compulsion to formulate a sense of personal identity. On the other side is the equally strong drive to stay connected to others. ICTs provide plenty of opportunities for meeting both needs.

No longer can computer users be described as antisocial hermits. These days, teens who are closeted in their rooms with their computers are not typically "alone" with the computer. They are often online with others. (See figure 4-2.)

FIGURE 4-2

Being physically alone does not mean being virtually alone.

They become part of a community by watching others, mimicking what they see, and finding ways to collaborate and share their expertise. The path is not always a smooth one. Others do not always let you in, and sometimes you do not want to participate. The news still seems to be full of stories about Internet addiction and about teens who are socially isolated because they spend too much time online. Early research pinpointed high use of the Internet leading to increased cases of teenage depression and declines in social support (Subrahmanyam et al. 2002). But ICTs have since become so prevalent and so inseparable from other forms of communication that all bets are off. It is time to revisit the role of the Internet in teenagers' social development.

Let Me In

Online life is rich with micro-communities, with opportunities to join, to affiliate, to belong. Some of these communities have the cachet of exclusivity. An individual must theoretically be invited by a current member to join Friendster.com, LiveJournal, an existing Yahoo group, and so on. Teenagers create community blogs for their groups of friends, and only members of the community can post and comment on them. These consciously created communities operate on the principle that "friends of mine are likely to be people you will like." There is also an implicit assumption of trust, that the people in the community are not axe murderers or otherwise unsavory characters.

Besides controlling membership and access, there are other, more subtle ways to define affiliation. Teenagers populate their IM profiles or signature files with in-jokes, quotes from one another, and running commentary on events that only a select few can appreciate. Teenagers tend to migrate to the blogging services their friends use, and on their own blogs they create links (or "friends lists") to one another's blogs. Nussbaum somewhat sarcastically notes that "the linked journals also form a community, an intriguing, unchecked experiment in silent group therapy—a hive mind in which everyone commiserates about how it feels to be an outsider, in perfect choral unison" (2004, 33). A less cynical take on this would be to observe that while teens want to retain their sense of identity as unique individuals, they also need to feel secure. Security comes from knowing that you are not so different from others, that you belong to the group, that you fit in.

Teens also typecast one another based on the blogging service they use. Certain services are associated with particular crowds, such as preppies, jocks, nerds, goths, or punks. The weblog example in chapter 3 reflects the lingo of ghetto/hip-hop culture. Part of identifying self and community lies in identifying who we are *not* like. But as social circles evolve and trends change, teens may switch blogging services in order to align with the community of the moment, the group that resonates with their current identity affiliation.

There are many other ways to express affiliations in the blog realm. Blogging services often offer features that promote community building. For example, LiveJournal users can select interests, which link to other LiveJournal bloggers who have identified the same interests. User-profile templates include places for name, birth date, gender, e-mail address, website URL, instant-message screen name, address, links to friends' LiveJournals and group blogs they have joined, and an open text box for writing a personal statement of the blogger's choice. Little of this information is required, and teen bloggers should be discouraged from using information that could identify them in real life. It is not even necessary to use one's real name. And most do not, instead using the space for creative self-expression, as they do with IM profiles. Bloggers also express affiliation by sharing or swapping content. Polls and questionnaires, accompanied by individual and group responses, tend to migrate from blog to blog within social circles.

Many teens join online communities with people they do not know in "real" life. As much as the Internet has a reputation for hosting sexual predators in chat rooms and the like, it is probably more likely that teens will find safe and healthy places to conduct their own social experimentation and information gathering. Online group space is a psychologically safe way to meet new people ("On the Internet, no one knows you're a dog"), as long as those relationships remain within the bounds of the virtual world and the community's focus. These forums come in many shapes—community blogs, web boards, and Usenet are just a few examples.

Today's teenagers do not seem to be Usenet devotees, though it is difficult to really know. Certainly among my students, web-based topical bulletin boards are more likely destinations when they are looking for specific information. One particularly tech-savvy student had this to say about his choice of website discussion boards over Usenet:

> [I haven't used Usenet] since the advent of online bulletin boards. . . . I think this is a case of trading freedom for security. Usenet is very much an unmoderated medium. It's completely open, freedom-of-speech stuff. On a web-based message board, you can expect messages to remain relevant to the topic and for people who act like jerks to be appropriately dealt with. While I'm sure this subdues discussion a little bit, most people seem to find it worth the trade off.

Here are a few ringing endorsements of web-based boards:

> I'm not into public chat spaces, but I go to a number of online bulletin boards, mostly related to a specific topic for information. In particular, the Woodwind.org message boards (and archives) are ridiculously useful to me as a clarinetist.

> i'll go to web boards if i'm having technology troubles and am looking for troubleshooting info, like when my sidekick went black and died. . . . those web boards saved it.

> I read and post to the online news service/message board Slashdot (at www.slashdot.org). I would be surprised if you haven't heard of it. This is great fun. In addition to learning something about computer news, I can post my thoughts for 700,000 people to see. It is an excellent, self-sufficient and interesting service, and their model for running the web board is one of the best that I have ever seen. I have never—yet—been flamed, but this is because I am polite. (normally)

Others are not so sure about the value of online forums as places to hang out:

> embarassingly enough i did this when i was younger (like 12 or 13) cause i thought it made me cool. when i realized that it was pointless and i didnt even WANT to meet any people from places like that i just stopped.

> i never do public chat rooms because my parents drilled it into me from the beginning not to do that. i guess i understand why

Let Me Out

Teens have a strong urge to share because it gives them a sense of belonging. At the same time, teens need privacy in order to protect a developing (and tender) sense of identity. There are two types of privacy in the context we are discussing. One is privacy within the online environment. There are times when one wants to share online and times when one does not. For teenagers, this duality is fraught with ambivalence, a pull-me, push-you tension. The other type of privacy that teenagers desire is protection from the adult world, from a world of outside authority. As noted earlier, ICTs afford teens protection from the prying eyes of adults.

Though teens want to be part of the group, sometimes they just need a break from being within reach, from performing. And sometimes they just need protection from interruptions when they are engaged in other activities. One student wrote to me:

> i usually am away when i have an away message up, but sometimes im just working on the computer and dont want to talk to someone who happens to be online then. it can be really annoying if youre trying to work and someone keeps talking to you.

One of my students opined that away messages, no matter what the tone or content, are used simply to convey the idea that "I'm away, please don't clog up my desktop with dozens of windows."

If teens do not want to be disturbed, why do they sign on and then make themselves unavailable? I am not alone in wondering about this:

> i dont do away messages. if im away i sign off of aim [AOL Instant Messenger]. i use it sometimes actually if im just off watching tv or something because if i left it on with no away message people might think i was being rude not talking to them. . . . theres some people though who NEVER sign off of aim and have to be using away messages all the time. its kinda ridiculous.

My theory about this phenomenon is that no one wants to be left out. At a minimum, one wants to be the proverbial fly on the wall and know who else is online. Here is another take on the subject:

> I usually use away messages so I can get some homework done. Every now and then, when I have a question to ask, I take off my message to see if anyone is online who can answer. I suppose I'm away, but not from my computer, just from the "talking zone."

I like the distinction this teenager makes between the literal truth and the real meaning of her action. Yet she does not actually sign off, which is telling. She chooses to remain connected, just not active. Teens can soften the appearance of their away state by composing apologetic or amusing away messages that explain their absence or induce feelings of sympathy in their would-be contacts. My son sometimes uses an away message that both invites contact and holds it at bay: "I am in front of my computer trying to do some work. Feel free to distract me." Nor does the content of the message have to reflect what one is actually doing:

> away messages can be a random statement of some sort, a quote from a song, a link. its only about half the time that they actually have something to do with where you are.

Get Them Out! Let Them In . . .

ICTs can also be used to exclude people from the community. Sometimes this use of technology is nothing more than teens controlling who they talk to and under what circumstances. It has become common to hide one's online presence and availability by using away messages to screen incoming inquirers, or by logging on with alternative screen names that are known only to a select few. Here is an away message, a bit more caustic than my son's, that one of my students sometimes uses:

> Things I might be doing:
>
> Making food
> Eating that food

Cleaning my room

HOMEWORK

Watching TV (while doing HOMEWORK)

Sitting here at the computer staring at you because you think I'm away but I'm
    NOT. Hahahaha.

One girl advised me of another strategy. "If you don't want to talk to anyone except one person you can put up an away message and go into a chat room with that one person and then people will leave you alone."

This exclusionary use of ICTs can have darker implications. For example, on IM it is possible to block individuals, which means that the person who is blocked simply cannot see that the blocker is online. Used judiciously, this tool is a benign way of keeping someone at arm's length (and an improvement over the days when we had to beg our parents to tell a caller we were not home). The blocking feature on IM can also be used more malevolently when social circles morph. Someone can be blocked temporarily, by one person or by an entire clique, but if blocked for too long that person will eventually figure out that he or she is the victim of a technological version of shunning. Online bullying, which will be discussed further in chapter 5, is also a growing concern.

On the other hand, it might be possible that ICTs elicit the softer side of the teen psyche as much as the meaner side. There is often a great deal of hand-holding and mutual encouragement. I read one girl's blog rant about an immature boy who had become "incredibly annoying." The subject of this boy's behavior passed from blog to blog, with a number of participants coming to his defense. One boy noted that the target's self-esteem was "nonexistent," and pleaded for understanding on his behalf.

Socializing

As play is a child's work, socializing is a teenager's work. Socializing is how teens learn to negotiate within the larger society, how they learn to learn the rules. All parents can recall the time of transition when they ceased to be the center of their children's lives, their places taken by their children's friends. This shift in focus is painful for parents, but is an essential part of growing up. Without it, young adults would not become mature adults, prepared to form their own family units (and to raise ungrateful children like themselves!). Through time, teenagers have found many ways to learn and practice these important socializing skills. New technologies probably allow them to practice to a fault, as reported by several of my students:

i have lots to say especially about aim because i waste my whole life online. i haven't done my homework for three days.

I waste a lottttt of time on aim talking to people.

The Internet is not the first technological environment to encourage social behavior or even to enable the formation of virtual friendships. Early telegraph operators swapped chitchat during slow times and developed their own shorthand vocabulary, which was not all that different in nature from the coded talk of today's online messaging environment (Joinson 2003). Romances were even known to develop over the telegraph. The codes and norms developed by telegraph operators, ham radio enthusiasts, and today's instant messagers are much more nuanced than would appear. Much information is exchanged in these terse, deceptively rich communiqués. As discussed at the beginning of this chapter, the social uses of communication technologies were never on the original drawing board. Developers viewed their inventions as business tools, survival tools, and tools for "serious" activity. But end users have never been particularly concerned if their use of a product fit the vision of its maker.

Teens have access to a variety of ICTs for connecting to their peers. Instant messaging software is probably the most popular tool, since it is generally free and so universally accessible. Madden and Rainie (2003) report that young adults and Internet veterans are among the most dedicated IM users, with teenagers "the most fervent IM users of all" (28). There is a bit of a chicken-and-egg question here too. Teenagers may drive IM traffic, but they are also driven by it. Grinter and Palen (2002) found that teenagers experience high and sustained IM use because of a desire to conform as well as to increase their socializing opportunities. In other words, if you are not online, you are "out." You miss not only the social experience but the chance to plan group social events. Those who are not online become invisible and their social capital suffers.

Online communication among teens shares some fundamental characteristics with face-to-face teenage communication. It is filled with the same drama, complexity, and import. Only the medium is different. Lewis and Fabos (2000) describe the experiences of Sam and Karrie, two teenage girls who use IM extensively. Both girls feel that IM is important in defining their social status. They manipulate their standing in a number of ways, such as adopting different language styles or adjusting the subject matter depending on who they are instant messaging with. Sam waits to respond to messages from popular people so she won't appear too eager, like a "loser." The assumption is that instant messagers are engaged in multiple simultaneous conversations, and she wants to appear just as engaged as everyone else. This behavior is not so different from tactics of earlier times—waiting to answer the phone until it has rung several times, not answering the door immediately, making a boyfriend wait a few minutes when he arrives for a date. Sam's choice to respond either promptly or slowly is just as calculated.

JARGON

Jargon has always been a way to establish credibility as a member of a community, to elevate one's status in it, or to unwittingly reveal one's utter cluelessness. We are all familiar with the typical shorthand of online speech—"lol" for laugh out loud, "imho" for in my humble opinion, "cya" for see you, "pos" for parent over shoulder (and something less savory, as well). In the online environment, the organic development of jargon is also influenced by mechanics and has a tendency to become ritualized. Here is a story from one of my students about the birth of one particular speech pattern:

> some time ago, when you wanted to say something loudly you'd say it and then add exclamation points by holding shift and "1" like so: !!!!!!!!!!!!!!!!
>
> but every so often, you'd let go of shift before you let go of "1" and get this: !!!!!!!!!!!!1111.
>
> then people started adding the "1's" intentionally. and now it has gone so far that people type: !!!!!!1111oneoneone

In similar fashion, certain misspellings become codified: "teh" is used for "the," "ist" (the German) for "is," and "pwn" for "own," (as in to defeat badly, usually in a game). Anyone who types these particular combinations of symbols, numbers, and letters is confirming an affiliation with a select few.

Certain stylistic conventions characterize online speech as well. One student sent me these examples:

> We also use asterisks to denote action. The text is in the third person:
>
> *wads up piece of paper and throws it into the trash*
>
> *blinks*
>
> *eats her sandwich slowly*

"Leetspeak" (from "elite") is a form of writing that uses numbers and symbols for letters; phonetic spelling; and the substitution of certain letters for others. Some terms are easy to decipher, like "d00d" for dude, or even "pr0n" for pornography. Others are more difficult—"ph33r |\/|y 1337 sk1llz" means "fear my leet skills."

Those who are adept online writers can communicate effectively and efficiently, even elegantly, using leetspeak. Those who are new at it or who are not sufficiently observant will make gaffes and lose status points in the online community. The overuse of certain conventions is as big a sin as their misuse. One of my students expressed his irritation this way:

> you may have noticed i'm fairly lax about grammar online (particularly capital-ization). but things like StICky cAPs and webspeak (omg, ur so hott lol) and l33tsp34k (j00 iz n00b) [leetspeak (you are a newbie)] annoy the hell out of me. i've found that in most forums and many blogs there are always a few morons who use one or more of the above, along with other annoying habits like TYPING IN ALL CAPS.

WHAT'S REAL, WHAT'S NOT

Instant messaging conversations are ephemeral. Unless someone deliberately saves a session or copies it, it disappears forever when the window is closed. On IM, it is easier for shy teens to flirt and for the inarticulate to do things that are difficult to do in person, such as break up with a boyfriend or girlfriend. The fleeting nature of IM also makes it easier for teens to be rude, to tease, and to bait one another. It is not always easy to tell what is truly meant and what is the game of IM banter. For example, AIM instant messaging allows one user to "warn" another if that person is being objectionable or offensive in some way. After an individual's warning level has exceeded a certain threshold, he or she is no longer able to send messages until a system-determined period of time has passed. One of my students told me that he and his friends sometimes have "warning wars"

> where we all gang up on each other and get warning levels really high. it's your online ammunition. it's all in good fun. and aim is a completely separate world anyway. . . . they may hate you on aim but it's still all cool in the real world. . . . cuz no one knows how you really feel on aim. with no facial expression and into-nation and so on.

Teenagers must learn the drill—when to take actions seriously, when not to, when things cross the line. Based on responses from my students, most seem to have these distinctions well in hand:

> I've had all kinds of arguments and fights over e-mail and instant messaging services. I block people, I warn people, I've been blocked, I've been warned—both for fun and more seriously. It's the nature of instant messaging.

> I think blocking and warning can either mean a lot or absolutely nothing. There are lots of times where I've been warned because my friends are trying to make points. It's not ill intentions, it's kind of attention-grabbing. However, if there are

people you only talk to online, it tends to get kind of dangerous if you block or warn the person. Since it's your only way of communication, it makes the matters a lot worse.

Every so often someone I don't know just starts talking and DOESN'T STOP. I block them.

I've never been warned for real but sometimes my friends will warn me just for fun. its kind of stupid actually. Once someone IMed me but I didnt notice because I was working on something else and since I didnt reply the person warned me up to around 70%.

Is this type of social interaction so different from real-world teenage social jockeying? Perhaps the tools are different, but the patter is the same.

PRIVACY AND INTIMACY

ICTs make some communications seem more ephemeral than they actually are. As a warning to our students, we tell them the following story when they are first issued school e-mail accounts. One of our teachers once noticed a piece of paper tacked to the bulletin board in the computer lab. It was a printed copy of an e-mail message in which a boy sheepishly asked a girl to go with him to a school dance. The teacher happened to notice that the boy was sitting in the computer lab and handed him the paper. The boy looked at it blankly for a moment, then pointed to the date at the top of the message. He had written the e-mail message two years earlier. Somehow, this message had survived the two years and then been printed and posted in a public place. It could have just as easily been forwarded electronically.

Just as e-mail communication is not truly private, the breakups, fights, and other dramas that are reported on blogs suddenly become community property. Discussions and dissensions hop blogs, and before long everyone has a vested interest in the outcome. There is also a tendency to overanalyze entries, with people looking for themselves in the subtext. One girl told me this story:

blogs are really good for telling people stuff without having to do it directly and without people really knowing. but sometimes people overanalyze. like once i was listening to a song by the white stripes. . . . the song is jack white singing to and about holly and holly singing to and about jack white. so i said something like "and who is this holly that jack white keeps talking about?"

and then my friend jake, who was sort of involved with a girl named holly at the time, said : "am I jack white? and if so, why do I have a codename? I'm fairly sure that I am but have no idea whatsoever of the significance of this; i'm pretty interested to find out though." so then i posted the lyrics to the whole song so he'd get the picture. which i didnt like doing. it was way too obvious and i like to be more cryptic. but it's really easy to seem too full of one's self when responding to blog posts that one imagines are aimed towards oneself.

I had other strong reactions from students to my questions about blogs:

i for one do not blog. i think that its kinda weird to be putting all of your feelings out for everyone to see. i keep a journal of my own and thats how its gonna stay. i would just always be afraid that people were reading it who might be offended by what i say or if i said something not nice about someone it would get back to them. this has happened to a couple people on several occasions and it wasnt very pretty. spilling your guts to the world through the internet is just a little odd to me. *other peoples blogs* on the other hand . . . i looooove to read other peoples blogs for the same reasons that i dont want my own. they're FULL of gossip. people will say things about other people that you might not have realized before. some people will also say things like "i have a secret!!!" and then if you grill them for long enough or dig back through previous blogs you can usually figure it out. they're really entertaining and theres three or four that i read religiously because the way they're written is funny and the content is usually veeeeery juicy. :-D

I've found that some blogs create an incredible amount of conflict and drama. A [name of different school] friend of mine and her friends are currently coming under fire from various "anonymous" classmates who leave comments criticizing the content of their blogs, specifically entries mentioning a particular student who has harassed them throughout the year and is currently threatened with expulsion for her behavior. All kinds of accusations get flung around, but the ones that i found strangest and hear a lot is "why do you care what i write here anyway?" "why does she bother you if you think she's stupid?" "you must be really pathetic to bother to read my comments/posts when you obviously don't like me/don't agree with me." these all strike me as dumb, because *of course* everyone involved is interested. We're teenagers. We find social conflict interesting, and no one should bother to deny it.

I was surprised and moved, however, to hear another side of the blogging picture, one that echoes the behavior of the students who defended the "really annoying" boy.

blogs are usually places for personal reflections, to talk about what's happened in one's day, new events, new things, new places. in one of my classes the other day we were discussing blogs, and the teacher said that they thought blogs were a lot like slam books—places to say nasty things about people that you wouldn't say to their faces. actually, that's not true. the blogs ive read rarely say a lot of negative things. people are too aware of how many other people might read it. its surprising how much people visit each other's blogs, but they do, and they'll get mad if they see their name in a bad light. i've found that blogs tend to be written in a style completely different from what the person's actually like. people reveal a lot of insecurities on their blogs, about how they're shy, lonely, depressed. . . . i think the main reason that blogs are written and read is that its interesting to see a whole new side of someone you thought you knew, and that its exciting to share that side with people.

I am more addicted to blogging and the blogs of other people than I'd like to admit. though i don't update my own very often, i find that i learn an incredible amount about my classmates from their blogs. there are a lot of people in my class that i used to write off as one stereotype or another, but when i found their blogs i was so surprised that they felt and thought things that i never imagined they would. here is the little epiphany i wrote in *my* blog: "i had no idea i had so much in common with my classmates. i go along and write people off because i think i know them. [person] is a suck-up prep, [person] is a greasy pervert, [person] is a hardcore nerd. but then i read their blogs and relate to what they write, and i think what a shame it is that I'm not friends with these people in real life."

Perhaps the real question to ask about ICTs is what they have meant for the *quality* of interpersonal communication. Are teens substituting shallower online friendships for in-person, higher-quality relationships? What good is it to have an online relationship that achieves a level of ease or intimacy that cannot be replicated in real life? Teenage boys, for example, may be more willing to be sweet or open online, and then clam up at school. There is also a difference between online-only relationships and relationships in which online communication supplements telephone calls and physical time spent together. A friendship that flourishes in multiple environments is bound to be more robust. And what about those blogs? Just because teens share their innermost secrets on a blog, are they getting the kind of feedback and support they would get from face-to-face interactions? On the other hand, would teen bloggers who are suffering from depression share in person what they write online? It's hard to say. As noted earlier, some things are lost and some are gained with the use of new technologies. It will be some time before we understand their implications.

Collaborating

One tried-and-true method for achieving a sense of community is by collaborating with others toward the attainment of a common goal. There is little doubt that the online environment facilitates collaboration. For example, instant messaging is commonly used to support schoolwork. Students may have conversations open while they work through math problems together. They initiate conversations to work on group projects, clarify assignments, check answers, discuss readings, and prepare for tests.

> often we make study guides before tests by opening a chat window and writing IDs (i.e. definitions, little snippets of information, etc. that we think will be on the test). Someone copies everything and formats it so we all have something to study.

Sometimes the chat environment is not the most productive or efficient one:

> there are often pre-test chat rooms. a great idea, doesn't always work though because we just end up joking around. then people have to branch off into the "real test chatroom."

Teenagers quickly learned to use group IM chat sessions for organizing offline events, online study sessions, and the like. No more inefficient and annoying telephone tag. Online "meetings" can be held when teens are unable to get together in person because of distance, transportation, or because meeting times are outside the normally permitted gathering time for a teenager.

FILE SHARING

A less "productive" example of ICT-enabled collaboration is file sharing, which generally connotes illegally swapping copyrighted music. Incomprehensible as it may seem to those of us who still regard the Internet as the radical new kid on the block, the "regular" Internet is now mainstream, populated by corporate and commercial interests. In contrast, peer-to-peer (P2P) networks are part of the Darknet, the Internet's unofficial underground of technologies and networks that enable the distribution of copyrighted (and other) material. Teens have a great deal of sympathy for the file-sharing movement, which operates outside the standard power structure. As minors, teens' rights are limited. They cannot vote, their ability to earn is restricted, and they simply do not have the control over their lives that adults enjoy. A system that flourishes independently of the status quo is very appealing to those who are otherwise bound by it.

P2P networks are decentralized grassroots endeavors based on egalitarian participation (assuming, of course, that the participants have access to adequate computing equipment and high-speed networks). Teens are treated as full partners in the P2P realm, without the stigma of their usual second-class citizenship. The relationship between users and hosts is typically personal and social, which is what teens are all about. So despite the legal and ethical problems associated with file sharing, teenagers are naturally drawn to these networks. The difference is that teens are now establishing connections with people they do not know, and joining an invisible community of like-minded people. This experience is evident in the e-mail one boy sent me about his use of IRC (Internet relay chat), a long-standing chat tool which also supports file sharing.

> im almost always using irc. if u dno, irc is a public chat environment that sup-
> ports the sharing of files. much of this is illegit, but i just use it to talk to ppl about
> certain things, because i find that the ppl there are really good at assisting me w/
> somn i dno about wit computers, or suggesting good bands.

I will have more to say about teenagers and file sharing in chapter 5.

GAMING

"Gaming" no longer means one kid sitting in front of one electronic device play-ing a solitary game. In confessing his own online gaming seduction experience, *Infoworld* columnist Chad Dickerson (2004) claims that systems such as Xbox pro-vide extremely rich collaboration environments that deserve close watching by business managers. Games can now be played online with friends as well as strangers, across wide physical distances. Players establish lists of "trusted friends," similar to buddy lists in instant messaging. Friends can then immediately see who is online and available for real-time play. Games, of both the interactive and sin-gle-player variety, are now more popular than television or movies for many teenagers (*Newsweek* 2003). Gaming, however, is not pervasive in the way instant messaging is, particularly among girls. It appeals to a smaller but highly dedicated group of aficionados.

Massively multiplayer online games (MMOG) and a subgenre, massively multiplayer online roleplaying games (MMORPG), are particularly suited to col-laborative sensibilities. An up-to-date listing of them, astonishing in its depth and range, is available from the Multiplayer Online Games Directory at http://www.mpogd.com/. Multiplayer gaming is the ultimate environment for establish-ing virtual friendships and a sense of community with people you have never met. One student told me about the many friends he has made and how he belongs to several "clans." "i can join a game in ravenshield and ppl are like 'yo [user name]!! hows it going?'" Gamers tend to identify with one genre or another, rarely cross-ing over. This particular student favors strategy games and first-person shooter games. Role-playing game (RPG) devotees are equally loyal in their affiliations.

The psychological dimensions of online game playing are complex and are fodder for many books and articles. Role-playing games provide a means of exploring identity and experimenting with or "trying on" different personas. Unless taken to extremes, RPGs are a safe way to immerse oneself in a fantasy world, to achieve (virtual) power, and to exert control in a world of one's own making. Online strategy games, however, are designed more for team building and collaboration than they are for personal identity exploration. One student told me that "If I want individual glory in my games, I'll play a nice peaceful game of Civilization [an off-line game] instead."

In many game environments, as a novice gains competence, play typically becomes more difficult and increasingly dependent on group collaboration. Each milestone is therefore much more of a team effort, resulting in a sense of belonging that some teens find rare in their real-world lives. But players can find it difficult to leave games because they have developed virtual obligations to one another (Valenza 2003a). At the same time, they are concerned about being "outleveled" while they are away. One of my sons told me that online gamers tend to specialize in just one game because there are simply not enough hours in the day to become competitive at more than one. Online game playing also has a reputation for becoming addictive. The game and the relationships developed through the game can become more important and satisfying than one's real life. Players of EverQuest, called "EverCrack" in its heyday, were sometimes known to buy and sell digital items on online auction sites like eBay. Each item represented many, possibly hundreds, of hours of play time.

BEYOND FALLOUT

There is a great deal about ICT-enabled life that is less than desirable. On one end of the spectrum is the merely annoying, and on the other end is the outright abhorrent, which will be examined more closely in the next two chapters. There are plenty of items to list under the "merely annoying" end of the continuum. Much online conversation is vapid. Teenagers waste a lot of time on instant messaging. They flame with the best of the old-timers. They have warning wars. But if the Internet disappeared tomorrow, these behaviors would find other homes; indeed, they have sprung from previous homes. On the other hand, ICTs also have enormous potential for enhancing teens' lives and helping them mature into interesting, productive adults. But it is up to them to decide if that is how they will use the tools.

From Mischief
to Mayhem
Behavior

I remember a disciplinary case at our school in which two students illicitly gained system administrator-level access to the computer network. The students were shocked to find themselves called in for remedial action because they felt they had not "done" anything—they did not change settings, delete files, or otherwise tamper with the system. In their minds, it was all about seeing if they could crack the system and poke around a bit. The process was their goal, as was the subsequent gloating. But since they did not technically break anything, why should they be in trouble? Indeed, they felt they had done the school a favor by finding the security holes in the network. This story raises two questions in my mind:

Is the Internet an intrinsically different environment from other shared human environments? In other words, does the Internet introduce a uniquely new moral sensibility?

What is it about adolescence that makes teens particularly prone to unethical online behavior?

Internet observers note important distinctions between Internet-*related* moral issues and Internet-*dependent* moral issues (Van Der Hoven 2000). Internet-*related* issues are those in which the moral issues are the same as they would be in parallel, off-line contexts. Downloading other people's files or e-mail is an invasion of privacy, morally identical to going through others' desk drawers or postal mail. Internet-*dependent* issues are actions that cannot occur without the Internet, yet the underlying ethical issues are familiar and perennial. Without the Internet, there would be no viruses, no spamming, no flame wars, and no hacking. But not all Internet users engage in these behaviors. The Internet offers unique opportunities for unethical behavior, but does not *require* its users to be unethical. The options for making moral choices exist as much on the Internet as they do in other arenas of human endeavor.

Technology innovators often deny or ignore the ethical implications of their work. Mary Shelley's Frankenstein story is a seminal example of how literature richly captures these morality tales. Dr. Frankenstein did not consider the consequences of his actions aside from the contributions he believed he was making to the advancement of scientific knowledge. Consumers of scientific knowledge, in their turn, leave technical development to the experts, effectively abandoning their own role in making moral choices. A student of mine once remarked that if music is "on the Internet," it is fair game for downloading—dismissing the circumstances that might have put it there. The fact of the technology seems to mean that subsequent actions are allowable, even intended.

Many of the moral issues we are now dealing with are not new, but have taken on new dimensions. Specific features of ICTs, like anonymity and speed, inject unfamiliar characteristics into conventional situations. Hamelink (2000) anticipates that genuinely new moral questions will eventually arise, particularly in the area of artificial intelligence and other intelligent systems. For example, what lies in store for human interaction with virtual beings? Who will be responsible for decisions made by intelligent digital assistants? For the time being, however, uniquely new moral issues are not at the heart of our problems. Instead, we are revisiting old moral dilemmas, made more complicated by new technologies.

Why does it seem that teenagers are especially susceptible to the lures of cyber-misbehavior? During adolescence, individuals formulate moral perspectives on many aspects of life. But intellectual growth often outpaces moral development. Psychologists and educators have long puzzled over minds that are so capable of knowledge absorption, yet relatively undeveloped in the subtler skills of moral judgment and decision making. Sociologist Émile Durkheim (1925/1961) believed that morality grew from attachment to a group and respect for its rules and symbols of authority. His views influenced behaviorist psychology and gave rise to the character education movement, associated most strongly with William Bennett.

In contrast, psychologist Jean Piaget (1932) believed that children define morality by actively struggling with issues of fairness. He felt that education should focus on ways of thinking about moral issues such as justice and human rights, methods of relating to others, and strategies for *choosing* what is moral. Piaget's theories belong to the cognitive-developmental traditions of thinkers like

John Dewey, and his work prompted the influential psychologist Lawrence Kohlberg's research into the stages of cognitive-moral development (1958, 1984).

MORAL DEVELOPMENT AND ICTS

A great deal of what we now understand about adolescent behavior in the online world comes from these theoretical perspectives. The rules we establish to maintain order are influenced by behaviorist psychology. Rules give adolescents clear boundaries and expectations, which they need to understand their place in the world. Codes of conduct, more nuanced than rules, reflect the cognitive psychology tradition, as they parse out the differences between truly immoral behavior (e.g., stealing credit card numbers) and mere violations of social convention (e.g., using all capital letters in an e-mail message). Nancy Willard's significant work on moral development in cyberspace reflects these traditions and more. She identified four key factors that influence online misbehavior (1998, 217):

Lack of affective feedback and remoteness from harm. The user does not see the hurtful impact of his or her actions, leaving him or her with an impression that there is none. This perspective is a result of not actively engaging in consideration of issues of fairness and justice.

Reduced fear of risk of detection and punishment. Negative consequences of unethical behavior are less likely in the Internet realm and therefore do not act as a deterrent. The user fears the consequences of getting caught, but does not acknowledge the moral rationale behind the rules and regulations.

New environment means new rules. Users rationalize that "real-world" concepts and values do not have any standing in cyberspace. Therefore, rule violations are seen as violations of (unimportant) social conventions, not of universal moral principles.

Perceptions of social injustice and corruption. Users justify unethical behavior by claiming they are righting the wrongs of the world and shifting the balance of power away from the corrupt "haves" to the "have-nots." Context mitigates the moral implications of actions.

Cyberspace is a ripe landscape for situational ethics, with people using technology to act as agents for solving personal and social problems. In the face of constantly shifting social conventions and norms, it is increasingly difficult for users to discern underlying moral values. Instead, "everyone does it" has become the operational mantra of the day.

TROUBLE IN CYBERSPACE

What are some of the behaviors and situations that typify trouble unique to cyberspace? Most of these technological hot spots have been covered extensively by the media. They are numerous and, like all things connected with the Internet, subject to change. This chapter examines some of the most prominent and troublesome of them, with a focus on how they are perceived through the lens of adolescence. The adolescent perspective is illustrated in this chapter by a series of examples that contain excerpts of students' responses to hypothetical cyberethics dilemmas. I extracted these nuggets from students' online responses to the ethical dilemmas posed in a unit of our school's required computer literacy course. I believe they are a good representation of how many teenagers respond to the morally ambiguous cyberspace landscape. (For a current listing of the scenarios that have been used in this curriculum, see http://www.uni.uiuc.edu/library/computerlit/scenarios.html.)

PARTY ON

Lester sends e-mail to the entire student body inviting them to a BYOB party at his house while his parents are out of town. He receives a message from a system administrator calling him in for a meeting with school officials. Lester objects because he feels that his e-mail is his own private business.

I agree with Lester in that it is his own business and the school shouldnt be checking emails for party invitations. If he hosts a party and his parents arent there, let him get in trouble with his parents, not the school. the school is not supposed to control your life outside of school.

He could have emailed over a non-school email service-provider account such as yahoo. He is old enough to take care of himself and judge what is right or wrong for him.

IT WAS A DRINKING PARTY!!! The kids are around our age! Plus, he sent it to the whole school, it was not private.

Well, if he sent the e-mail to the whole school, it's not his own business; it's everyone who received its business. Even though the System Admin didn't receive the message, it would be assumed that lots of people would receive it. Also, by using the school network, the user has already agreed to allow the administrator to view his/her files if a need arises.

This is illegal if hes too young, and still not right if his parents dont know. They arent even home, and they have no idea what their son is doing while they are away. Hes drinking, and hes inviting others to come to his house w/o his parents knowing, to drink and party with him! sending school emails is NOWHERE close to this violation.

Cheating

The popular perception is that if teenagers are not looking at pornography on the Internet, then they are using the Net to plagiarize schoolwork or download copyrighted music. Plagiarism has certainly been made easier by the Internet. Students can copy and paste from many sources; they can also download prewritten or customized term papers (often at outrageous prices). Teachers fight back in a number of ways. They collect in-class writing assignments so they will have original writing samples for comparison. They use search engines to find unique strings of words from suspect papers, and they use the services of companies like Turnitin.com, which conduct more exhaustive searches for evidence of plagiarism. Teachers also retool assignments to make them more immune to plagiarism. A student who has to write an imaginary dialogue between two philosophers will have more difficulty plagiarizing her paper than if she is assigned to write a traditional comparison of the two philosophers' perspectives.

David Callahan's book *The Cheating Culture* (2004) sets this behavior in the context of a larger societal trend. From his extensive data gathering, he concludes that cheating has become an American way of life. He blames the competitive economy and the fact that most cheaters are neither caught nor punished. In other words, crime *does* pay and, furthermore, puts those who do not participate at a distinct disadvantage. Many people who consider themselves law-abiding and honest citizens find themselves slipping into cheating in small ways, whether by fudging a bit on their tax forms, exaggerating their children's accomplishments for a competitive admissions process, or failing to return incorrect change at the grocery store. The everyone-does-it mentality is so seductive that cheating and other forms of small-time dishonesty have lost their aura of disrepute.

Improper Use of Intellectual Property

The old-time Internet ethos purports that information "wants" to be free. The open source movement, in which computer code is made transparent and available to the public for modification and improvement, is a reflection of this perspective—that anything worth creating is worth sharing. Hamelink opines that "CyberSpace is one enormous photocopying machine" (2000, 157) and reminds us that copying intellectual work has an honorable heritage:

> Bach copied and reworked music made by others and did this with great respect, creativity and innovation. Many of his choral melodies were taken from other composers. If copyrights were indeed very strictly enforced, jazz musicians would be in deep trouble. In line with the current regime jazz legend Bill Evans should

have copyrighted his brilliant harmonic discoveries and any time somewhere in the world a pianist used his way of playing a B flat chord, money would have to be paid to Evans' publisher or record company. (Hamelink 2000, 161)

It does not help that modern copyright law and its enforcement have become so draconian that many people find it easy to excuse law-breaking behavior. The prevailing tension is reminiscent of the early days of VCR technology, when Hollywood moguls feared the demise of their studios once consumers abandoned theaters for the comforts of home and bootlegged videos. The industry found a way to accommodate marketing practices to the new technology, and now video and DVD rentals account for a sizable portion of their profits. Presumably, a similar scenario is in store for the newer forms of entertainment technology. Still, there is not much use in taking a cavalier attitude toward copyright law, or at least toward its intent. Creators deserve the right to make a living from their work. It is easy to claim that the recording companies are the "bad guys" and deserve to be cheated, but such excuses are often covers for other, less noble motives. The fact remains that downloading or file sharing copyrighted material is currently against the law.

LET'S DANCE

Roberta and Todd are the DJs for the next school dance. They surf the Web for their favorite MP3s and download several songs, which they burn onto a CD to play at the dance. Some of the songs are from big name groups and others are from new artists who are using the Web to build an audience.

I actually don't see anything wrong with this. I have bought CDs because of mp3s, not the other way around. The rich people have enough money, and the other small groups are doing mp3s because they want recognition.

I don't agree with this, because you should not be able to download music for free without permission. No music should go unpaid.

While you may not agree with it, it's going to occur anyway. It's too big of a phenomenon to be stopped in its tracks, and the more we resist it, the more people are going to partake in it.

It makes people come to know and love the music more and isn't that what music is all about? It is about people enjoying music not about money. I pity those who do think that money is what music is about because they are the people who miss the beauty of it.

Teens are among the most prolific users of file-sharing software, which has become a primary means of acquiring music without having to pay for it. The concept of ownership of intellectual property is a particularly difficult one for them to grasp. They see no reason to protect the body of intellectual work they might have created by this point in their lives. So why should others mind? Instead, creators should be gratified that others appreciate their work enough to want to have it.

Hacking

The unadorned, original meaning of the term "hacking" is merely this: clever programming, a willingness to share it, and an appreciation of the same talent in others. But the term has assumed other associations in the public mind. Many confuse it with the more malevolent "cracking," which is invasive and destructive. Hacker ethics has its roots in Willard's third factor, that the online environment signifies new rules and codes of conduct. The new code of conduct values the sharing of expertise and information. There are, of course, many shades of difference in hacker ethics. Some feel that it is perfectly acceptable to break into systems for purposes of exploration and learning, as long as no vandalism or breach of confidentiality occurs. Others regard this attitude as gussied-up cybervandalism.

"Hacktivists," aggressive and purposeful in their outlook, view the end as justifying the means, particularly when they act out of a strong sense of moral obligation to an overarching cause. For example, it is not uncommon for activist-minded groups or individuals to expose transgressors, publishing names and descriptions of wrongdoing. Here is an example from a website called *Hackers against Child Pornography* (http://members.tripod.com/~ListedBlack/index2 .htm):

> I place this web page up because I will be exposing those who partake in this sick garbage and I want the world to see who these morons are. I personally am going to wipe out any computer that contains child pornography and I could care less about law at this point. The law enforcement is going to do SHIT about this and its up to us to do what we can to help clean up this god-forsaken planet! Law Enforcement wont do anything and the Government turns their heads at it. . . . Its time to put a stop to this abuse! Below you will find data about the assholes who partake in child pornography.

These Robin Hood-style vigilante tactics are similar to those used by other extreme-leaning activists, from ecoterrorists to political advocates of various stripes. Hacktivists may deface political websites, initiate denial-of-service attacks, or even impersonate and subvert an opponent's online identity.

The hacker ethic holds particular appeal for computer-savvy adolescents, who savor the sense of power and entitlement that seems to come with the territory. They see it as their obligation to test the limits of online systems by finding security weaknesses and otherwise dabbling in spaces where they are not authorized to be. School administrators now find themselves engaged in "nerd discipline," and are confronted with a troublesome mind-set that seems to defy standard corrective approaches. Perpetrators regard school computing rules as applying only to others (who are idiots and need to be controlled), not to themselves (who are brilliant and should be paid to take care of the system).

HACKING

Marla figures out that when she is logged into the school network, she can look at others' directories, make copies of files, and deposit new files. The UNIX operating system was designed to allow this functionality so that programmers could share their work. Mr. Klausinsky objects when he observes Marla poking around in another student's directory. But Marla responds by saying, "If the system allows me to do it and there's no specific rule against it, what's the problem?"

This is an example of hacking. Hacking is illegal. Marla should lose all of her computer privileges.

No, she shouldn't lose all of her computer privileges. She should be reprimanded, but nothing more. There is no rule against it, and this kind of hacking is not really illegal. Technically, she hasn't done anything wrong, because there's no rule against it and no one has told her she can't do it. She should just be warned that if she ever does it again, expulsion or something. Maybe they should make a new rule about UNIX saying not to explore others' directories.

It doesn't matter whether or not there is a rule against it, rules are not always up to date, and a student should listen to their conscience.

There is a rule, despite what Mrs. Harris says, and the system administrator WAS VIOLATING THEIR CONFIDENTIALITY by not protecting users' directories by default. Marla was just taking advantage of incompetence/corruption by viewing files that she and everyone else were given permission to view . . . This is a quote from Mrs. Harris's message, which you were supposed to read: "The Unix operating system was designed to allow this functionality." And that quote is true.

There may be no specific rule against it, but you shouldn't go poking into it anyway. And just because the system allows you to do it doesn't mean you should. There are all kinds of things the system allows you to do which you shouldn't.

In Van Buren's (2001) exploration of high-school hacker ethics, the students she interviewed revealed numerous ways they could wreak havoc, including bringing the entire school network to a halt. Their focus was on the potential power of their actions, the fact that they *could* cause damage but did not. When asked point-blank how poorly funded institutions could solve problems of network security, they had no suggestions. Their counterargument was that most student hackers, like themselves, were not malicious, offering "the fact that nothing serious had happened to the school networks as evidence of their peer groups' beneficent nature" (Van Buren 2001, 69). The possibility that they, or other like-minded individuals, engaged in immoral behavior was not a notion worth considering.

Some teen hackers, though, have no qualms about mischief-making, either for its own sake or for more malevolent purposes. Online identity theft is a good example of this mind-set. Simple impersonation can easily occur when someone forgets to log off a networked computer and another sends out e-mail in that person's name, alters files, or otherwise tampers with the account—often just to "teach the loser a lesson." Or an account can truly be hacked, using deliberate means for a variety of malicious purposes. In either case, not only has the victim's personal space and information been invaded, but his or her identity has been assumed and misrepresented.

Freedom of Expression versus Freedom from Expression

The Internet has introduced unrivaled opportunities for personal expression, but these opportunities are not without cost or conflict. One person's right to free speech is a potential invasion of another person's privacy. Speech can be hurtful, even if accidentally so. Children first learn that they are never to lie. Later, they come to understand that utter honesty is not always the best policy, that there is a time and place for every expression. But the facelessness of online communication removes inhibitions, making it easier than ever to speak before thinking, disregarding or minimizing your target's reactions. Sensitivity to others' feelings has taken a back seat to the efficiency of the send key. The phenomenon of flaming is an interesting case of "offensiveness deflation." No one complains much about flame wars anymore, teens least of all. They are unlikely to be punished for flaming of the worst kind, let alone fingered for the garden-variety rudeness that is so common in instant messages. If warning wars on IM elicit little response, then how can ordinary insults?

All these factors make it easier to use ICTs as tools to violate or betray confidences. Grinter and Palen (2002) report the concerns teens have about IM conversations among friends being saved or copied, and then shown to others. Teens therefore view the phone as being a safer medium for exchanging sensitive or confidential information. Blogs have also raised the stakes on the impact of gossip. And of course, the ability to save, forward, or alter private e-mail can be debilitating to those involved. One of my students commented:

> I've lately noticed how dangerous it is to try to have a serious conversation with somebody when you don't know how closely they value the information that goes on between you two. I mean, if you type it and send it to the person, that means they can save it and show it to someone else or copy and paste. It makes any committing words a serious hazard to your privacy. Just because they say they won't, doesn't mean they won't. I don't know, AIM and E-mail give you incredible powers of invasion of privacy.

ICT speech can also be used to intentionally cause pain and discomfort. Teens have been known to (truthfully or falsely) "out" others by posting their names on sites like isgay.com. They can post their peers' and teachers' home tele-

---

POPULARITY POLL

Joe uses a web board to conduct a popularity poll. He asks, "Who are the people you like most in the sophomore class? Who are the people you like least?" A couple of names predominate on the "least liked" list. Suzy, who is one of those people, starts missing a lot of school. Her parents are puzzled because the doctor can find nothing physically wrong with her. School officials warn them that Suzy will have to repeat the year if her attendance doesn't improve.

I think Joe should have probably done something else for his poll. Some people would find the results offensive. What he could have done instead was just ask who people thought was popular, and not who was unpopular. That way the "unpopular" people wouldn't get their feelings hurt, and the people who were on the poll would be glad to see their name on the list.

I agree that they should take least popular off, but I think that the whole thing should be gotten rid of. It could still hurt people. It could get people talking and the "least likes" might get out.

I believe that Suzie has to talk to the other sophomores and find out why she is disliked. After that, the school should heavily punish the person who started the "popularity poll" in the first place, for creating such a thing. He should also get a lecture about creating situations that might be offending or hurtful.

I think that Suzy should receive some help and support and Joe should receive some kind of punishment for what he has done. If she explains why she has missed that much school, she shouldn't have to repeat the year.

phone numbers to sex-oriented public bulletin boards and newsgroups. And they create or add to websites that satirize or defame people they know, such as rate-myteachers.com, where students publicly critique their teachers. The subjects of these sites are not celebrities whose lives become something of public property, but ordinary citizens who should have more of an expectation of personal privacy.

SEPTEMBER 11

After the September 11 terrorist attacks, many students and teachers send related e-mails to the "all-student" or "all-faculty" mailing lists. Most of the messages contain information about the status of former students and about ways people can help in the crisis. But Penelope sends a long note with a heavy religious message. And Mr. Snidden sends out patriotic graphics and images. A small delegation of students takes their objections to the administration. They had understood that these all-school mailing lists, which are screened by the school's system administrator, were supposed to be used for school-related, informational purposes only.

I do not think that this is a good idea. It is probably against the law to send religious things on a school mailing list. Most people will just be annoyed by it, and it is inappropriate to try to convert people on a school server.

I agree. People will probably be annoyed with their inbox overflowing with messages that they may not care about. I don't think it's against the law to send religious things on a school mailing list, but people really shouldn't do that. Instead, they should inform people about their beliefs in a different way.

If you don't want to see the e-mail, just delete. If the all-school mailing lists were only meant for this then yes they should not have sent these messages. on the other hand it's the students choice whether or not to read and/or listen to what these say.

There is nothing wrong with the patriotic images, since we are all living in America and there should be American spirit in everyone. I can understand that religious messages might be found offensive, but we can deal with that. It is fine to express their complaints, just as it is fine to express feelings through emails, but the school email system is not for this purpose so Penelope and Mr. Snidden should have used a home email or something else to do this.

This situation is a difficult one. Everyone is right in some ways, and everyone is wrong. Although I think both Penelope and Mr. Snidden meant well and were doing what they thought was right, some people might be offended by their messages. However, everyone is entitled to freedom of speech, and so they should be able to send messages with their own beliefs and opinions. I'm really not sure what should be done in this situation because everyone is right.

An extreme case of how unfettered free expression can impinge on the rights of others occurred when a student, from his home, created a website called *Teacher Sux*. The site contained offensive and threatening comments about his principal and his algebra teacher, depicting the latter with her head severed and her face morphing into Adolf Hitler's face. The boy showed the site to other students at school, where it was subsequently viewed by the principal and the teacher in question. His parents sued the school district for suspending their son, claiming his constitutional rights were violated. The Pennsylvania Supreme Court ruled against them in *J. S. v. Bethlehem Area School District* (569 Pa. 638 2002; 807 A.2d 847 2002), finding that obscene and libelous speech was not constitutionally protected. Even though the site was created without the use of school computing facilities, the fact of its accessibility at school and the deleterious impact of its content was enough to convince the courts that irreparable harm had been done to those depicted and to the school climate.

Harassment and Bullying

Bullying is a plague that has long been an unfortunate feature of childhood and adolescence. Now with ICTs, bullying can go on twenty-four hours a day rather than being confined to the school day. The victim's home is no longer a place of escape and sanctuary. Rachel Simmons, author of *Odd Girl Out: The Hidden Culture of Aggression in Girls* (2002), reports that bullies tend to be products of the middle class. They engage in "alternative" or unconventional (i.e., nonphysical) aggression because their culture does not always allow them to display anger in a more open way. These same "good kids" lose their inhibitions and sense of accountability in the online environment, writing things they would never say to one another in person (Simmons 2003). Perpetrators can later behave as though nothing had happened, or even claim that someone else was using their screen name or e-mail account (claiming to be victims themselves).

School administrators are especially frustrated by the unique challenges of this particular battleground. First, they do not necessarily understand that an unsafe environment *at* school can be created *outside* of school (as the courts determined in the case of the Teacher Sux author). Second, precisely because most of these activities happen outside school, officials may not learn of the harassment and if they do, they lack the evidence required to pursue disciplinary action. It is difficult to establish a paper trail in an ephemeral online environment like instant messaging. Teens often share screen names and passwords, further complicating investigations. Finally, the pursuit of harassers may be inhibited by schools' fears of being accused of violating privacy rights.

As in the off-line world, many cases of harassment go unreported. Research commissioned by the Girl Scouts of the USA found that 30 percent of girls who were sexually harassed in a chat room simply left the chat room and did not tell anyone about their experience (*Girl Scout Research Institute* 2002). Another 28 percent got angry and wrote a nasty note back. But 21 percent said they did nothing because "it happens all the time" and "is no big deal"—a sentiment often expressed by both harassers and victims in parallel non-Internet situations. Only 14 percent told friends about the incident and just 7 percent told a parent. Why don't victims just block the abusers' screen names, ignore their text messages, and delete their e-mail? It is not so simple. If too many technical blocks and filters are in place, legitimate communication cannot get through. Most of all, the victim remains continuously aware of the abuser's presence. If a group of bullies is involved, the whispering and pointing has a virtual life as well as a physical one.

SYLVESTER'S WEBSITE

Word gets around that Sylvester maintains a website on the Geocities web server. Besides containing sexually explicit references about a couple of girls at school, the website links to hard-core porn sites. School officials find out about it and tell Sylvester that they plan to inform his parents about the website.

I think that the school should not notify the parents of the child. The incident did not happen on a school server. We're talking here about a Geocities server, where the school has no business reprimanding a student. I agree that what the student [did] was unacceptable, but I think that what the child does is his business is his/her deal, not the school's. The school has some business in the fact that a student was involved, but only if the student contacts the school. I think that the school has no right whatsoever to take action unless specifically requested by the student.

But the people that the site pertains to are at school. The parts of the site that involve the girls from the school are sexual harassment and should be dealt with. The school may not be able to prevent him from having the site, but they can deal with the problems from school. And I assume if he is harassing them online there may also be abuse at school.

The school does not have the right to tell the parents, the school has the responsibility to tell the parents that their child is upholding an inappropriate web site. The parents MUST BE INFORMED. They (the parents) do not have to take action, but they MUST know.

The school should not be involved, but the officials should probably be able to tell his parents, simply as some concerned people rather than as school officials. If they do not bring the school into it, but simply inform the parents of his website, shouldn't it be OK?

Access to Inappropriate Content

The potential ability to access online pornography and other questionable content is one of the most volatile Internet-based issues that schools and libraries have had to deal with. The problem is actually a much bigger one than the simple availability of pornography on the Internet. It has to do with minors' rights to access a wide variety of information, the conflicting and confusing content that is thrown at them by well-meaning as well as unscrupulous content providers, how types of information are interpreted by the community, and kids' personal ability to deal with what they are exposed to. Because these concerns are so broad and of such importance, the next chapter is devoted to their examination.

ANOREXIA

Several students have discovered a website that promotes anorexia as a lifestyle choice rather than as an eating disorder. The site includes tips for weight loss, pictures that glamorize the anorexic look, a discussion that board members use to support one another, and other materials that promote "anorexic pride." School counselors have asked that this site and others like it be blocked on the school network. They point out that anorexia is a deadly disease and that some students are particularly susceptible to this type of misinformation.

That website should definitely be shut down for good. Anorexia kills a lot of adolescent girls, and a website like that is obviously going to make them anorexic. The stuff on that website points out false information and can be deadly.

The school may block the website, but there still might be issues of accessing it at home. I believe that the school shouldn't block the website, but, instead, allow the students to make their own decisions on whether or not to trust the site.

I feel that the school is taking the right action. The school is responsible for the children while they are attending the school and anorexia could be very harmful to students and even deadly. The website in a way is brainwashing them and should be banned from the school network immediately

The school can use their own discretion on what sites they want available in their school. If students want to look at sites that are not permitted in the school computer they may look on their own time out of school.

If the school counselors blocked this site from the network, they would have to block all sites dealing with this topic. We must respect freedom of speech and accept there are many sites with inappropriate content on the web. It is not fair or efficient to block this site, and students would most likely simply find another site similar to it. Either the school [should] develop a system which generally blocks sites dealing with this topic, or not block it at all.

The Deep End

Content

C ontent, loads of it. The Internet has given us this gift. It is a wonderful gift, representing a transformation of the information landscape perhaps as profound as the invention of the printing press. Like many gifts, however, there is a catch. Not all the content is of high (or even reasonable) quality, and not all of it is what it appears to be. The onus is on the consumer to make wise choices, to pick out the worthy content from the onslaught of the crassly commercial, the suspect, and the unsavory. The focus of this chapter is on the implications of open access to online information of all types. I will examine the tactics used by the purveyors of questionable content to make it palatable, marketable, and ultimately acceptable to significant numbers of people, including (and maybe especially) teens.

Not all questionable content is equally questionable. For purposes of discussion, I have sorted this continuum of material into somewhat arbitrary categories, followed by a similar sorting of the variety of techniques used by content providers to persuade and manipulate. Ultimately, students need to be able to protect themselves by sharpening their media literacy skills and becoming savvy consumers of online information. Teaching these skills will be the subject of chapter 7.

DEFINING "INAPPROPRIATE"

First, it is important to acknowledge that terms like "questionable" and "inappropriate" have different meanings in different contexts. What is considered acceptable content at home may not be considered acceptable at school or in the workplace. Furthermore, there is disagreement about what constitutes inappropriate Internet content within formal schooling environments.

I appreciate the framework articulated by Doug Johnson (2003) in which he classifies the uses of technology in terms of place, audience, and purpose. *Place* is an issue of ethical resource allocation. Because the demand for technology has outpaced its acquisition, priority for its use must be given to academic needs. The inappropriate use of personal technologies also distracts from classroom activities. Cell phone use in schools, for example, may need to be prohibited to protect classroom learning. The issue of *audience* arises with concerns about the appropriateness of content. Johnson advises schools to define and teachers to help students understand the characteristics and conditions under which content becomes unsuitable for school use. Content and language that are used outside of school are not always appropriate in schools, where a wide range of value systems must coexist. *Purpose* has to do with how students use technology and how schools control that use. While schools must respect students' rights to personal expression and their explorations of identity, students must also understand when exercising those rights becomes harmful to themselves or others. Finally, Johnson reminds us that technology itself is neutral, that it can be used for constructive as well as destructive purposes.

Sometimes it is tempting to fall back on policies that are either easy to enforce or are implemented merely to prevent situations that are difficult to control. For example, educators can be awfully prescriptive about what students are allowed to look at online while at school. Many acceptable-use policies restrict *all* use of the Internet to academic purposes. The rationale for such policies can be a factor of limited computer resources, as Johnson notes, but I suspect it is at least as often a consequence of our own beliefs and prejudices about what students should be doing during school hours, in the school building, and, not inconsequentially, with taxpayer-funded resources. When a school board member is touring the school, it can be hard to justify a library scene in which students are browsing eBay, comparing stock prices, or checking the latest NFL scores. From the student point of view, however, restrictive policies lump nonacademic websites in with the truly odious—the pornographic, the violent, the hateful. It does not appear to them that their teachers and administrators draw any distinctions among these wildly disparate Internet-based resources and activities. They have only to look at the print resources in the school library that are *not* curriculum-related—the sports and car magazines, the teen girl magazines, even the fiction section—to have their impressions confirmed.

One way to combat this impression is to deliberately incorporate nonacademic content into the educational process, where its use might be supervised and mined for pedagogical purposes. The examples above—online auctions, stock portfolio analysis, sports scores—all present opportunities for mathematics and economics instruction, at the very least. Even presumed nonacademic services like chat, Usenet, and instant messaging can be put to academic use. In the next chapter, I will discuss such options along with techniques for teaching content evaluation. For now, suffice to say that highly restrictive access policies can block a huge range of web resources and Internet services, to the detriment of student learning.

Ultimately, schools and libraries must define the principles and standards that best fit their individual settings and circumstances. In my own case, practices have emerged from some underlying personal philosophies. First, students shall do no harm, either to themselves or others. Next, the Internet is provided at school for learning. Last, personal growth and identity exploration are components of learning. A couple of examples illustrate how these perspectives play themselves out. The first is my choice to allow students to use the computers in our library to pursue personal interests. David, who consults sports sites like ESPN (http://www .espn.com), is typical of these users. During baseball season, he navigates from ESPN's major league baseball scores pages to its message boards site. From there, he selects "MLB teams," then "Chicago Cubs." By following the Cubs message board, he keeps up with the news of his favorite team but, more importantly, he learns the banter of this (largely adult) community, discovers what is important to its members, and gains a more nuanced understanding of baseball issues than he might pick up from traditional news sources. Though David posts a question every once in a while, he generally confines himself to reading and learning. If David were a student at a school that restricts computer usage to curriculum-related purposes, he would not be allowed to further this aspect of his "education." From my perspective, as long as others do not need his computer for school-related work, David can continue to follow the conversations on these message boards as much as he likes.

While I defend the rights of the student who hones his baseball knowledge in my library, I prohibit computer gaming. Why this distinction? The difference lies in the impact of the activity on the environment around it. Unless it is carefully managed (which can be done, as will be discussed in chapter 8), gaming can turn the library, the computer lab, the classroom, into an arcade. The space becomes loud and raucous, and eventually even smelly from the close congregation of agitated bodies, usually male. No one else who wants to use the space for its intended purpose has a chance. Picturing the scene without computers makes the differences more obvious. The Chicago Cubs fan would be using magazines and newspapers to conduct his research (although, apart from the letters-to-the-editor section, those sources would not provide him with the community dialogue he finds on the message boards). The game players would be chasing each other around the library, wielding sound-enabled toy laser weapons. The ground rules are evident: learn, and do no harm.

QUESTIONABLE WEB CONTENT

Besides a lack of agreement about the role of nonacademic Internet activity and content in the school or library, there are differences of opinion about what constitutes questionable content. There is a big distinction between a hard-core pornography website and *Glamour* magazine's website, even though the *Glamour* site offers plenty of sex tips and is hardly a "wholesome" destination for a twelve-year-old. Many topics that were once vilified have become mainstream, erstwhile taboos have insinuated themselves into the popular culture, and alternative lifestyles are well-represented on the Internet. Though much of this content is suspect, as will be discussed, a great deal of it is useful, legitimate, and well-intentioned. The Internet has given curious teens the wherewithal to dabble or to dive wholeheartedly into the esoteric, the avant-garde, and the unusual.

Witchcraft is a good illustration of these changing mores. Though still a forbidden subject in some communities, witchcraft has otherwise become almost conventional, popularized by the Harry Potter books and by television shows like *Buffy the Vampire Slayer* and *Charmed*. Mattel even introduced a Secret Spells Barbie in the fall of 2003. Information about Wicca, the practice of witchcraft, has blossomed online. Teen Wiccans, most of them girls, congregate on the Internet, where they swap e-mails, ideas, and spells (Hagerty 2004). They flock to The Witch's Voice (http://www.witchvox.com/), a "proactive educational network" that lists more than 250 college groups and nearly 400 teenage groups. From those links, geographically isolated teen pagan practitioners can find community in groups like New Moon Grove (http://groups.yahoo.com/group/newmoongrove/), a "nonhostile meeting place for young Wiccans, Neopagans, or other open or like-minded people."

Beyond this middle ground, where debates about appropriateness flourish, is an undeniably scary world. There is little quibbling about the unsuitability of the Internet's seamiest side—the hard-core pornography, the violent imagery, the place of refuge for scoundrels and villains of all types. For a variety of reasons that will be discussed later in this chapter, much of this content is hard to immediately detect. Or it actually comes marching in uninvited, invading our private online space. For these reasons and more, it is important to understand the nature of the Internet's dark side. Let's start by taking a quick tour through some of these content types.

Spam and Company

At the more "benign" end of the Internet's underbelly is the unwanted content that arrives hidden in spam, pop-up advertising, spyware, and the like. Even public chat spaces are populated with "spim" harvesters, those who collect screen names and distribute the IM version of spam. It is one thing to go looking for trouble, but it is another to have trouble come marching in unbidden and unexpected. My students respond to these aggravations with relative equanimity: "Yeah, sometimes spammers send me porn links and stuff . . . it's so annoying." Reactions like this one tell me that the shock value of spam and spim has declined, as it has for flame wars. Instead, this generation has become accustomed to the intrusion and seems to regard it as a necessary evil.

As sanguine as my students may appear to be about these invasive phenomena, their impact is likely to have a lasting effect on the future of communication technologies. Spam is rendering e-mail nearly useless in some cases. The deluge is frustrating and resource-draining at the least, and outright destructive at worst. At whatever level, it takes the control out of users' hands.

Pornography

Ah, pornography, the Great Evil of the Internet. Our worries about it spring from two different areas of concern. First, we worry about intrusive pornography that arrives, like spam, without being summoned by the user. Online porn is more than accessible—it can sometimes actually be hard to avoid. As casual as teens may purport to be about invasive ICT phenomena, they are not always comfortable with it. I will never forget one particular eighth-grade research project on early man, assigned when we were relative newcomers to the Internet. The students who searched on the phrase *homo erectus* were rather stunned by the results lists that seemed to shout for attention from their screens.

Peer-to-peer networks have now become major conveyers of online pornography. Teens can unwittingly acquire hard-core video clips, many of which have innocuous file names or names similar to something they might be looking for. To document this problem, the General Accounting Office used Kazaa file-sharing software to search on popular names like "Britney," "the Olsen twins," and "Pokemon." Of the results, 56 percent included some type of pornography, 8 percent of it involving minors (Krim 2003). Teens do not need credit cards to share these files, nor does filtering software recognize or block them.

The second source of our worry about pornography has to do with our knowledge (and memories!) of the teenage mind. We all recognize that curiosity about sexuality is a normal part of growing up. When I was a teenager, boys were sneaking copies of their fathers' *Playboy* magazines and girls were reading contraband copies of *Peyton Place* to find out about sex. Nowadays, societal standards about sexual content in the public forum have loosened considerably, partly as a consequence of the mixed messages broadcast by today's media. Teens need look no further than the nearest billboard, grocery-store magazine rack, music video, Calvin Klein ad—or even the current cover of *Rolling Stone* in their school library—to find rather explicit sexual imagery. What was once taboo has become commonplace. Accessibility has dulled our shock meters, inevitably leading to new standards of acceptability.

Even though standards of sexual explicitness have relaxed, viewing hard-core pornography is still a stigmatized activity. The pornography industry has long taken advantage of technology to minimize the effects of that stigma. Videocassettes changed pornography access from a public affair to a private one, bringing it first to booths at the adult store and then to VCRs in the home. The Web provides this same privacy and convenience to teenagers, who are barred from the adult sections of video stores. The online environment reduces their fear of detection and encourages a sense of disinhibition. But the stakes are higher in the online environment because of the sheer availability of so much extremely explicit material. Online pornography can make *Playboy* and *Penthouse* look like *Good Housekeeping* magazine.

Crackpots, Wackos, and the Demons of Adolescence

Unfortunately, the Web is a mecca for old-fashioned and newfangled crackpots peddling questionable products, information, and solutions for all of life's ills. Curious teens will discover ideas and instructions for body piercing, tattooing, and branding. Troubled souls will locate plenty of information on weaponry, military equipment, and spy gear. Occult interests are easily satisfied by the plethora of websites on satanism, voodoo, and demonology. The information found online about over-the-edge topics is by no means monolithic in opinion, tone, or intent. While perusing a discussion forum on tattooing, I was amused to read the outraged comments of principled tattoo artists condemning the "scabwrenchers," "scratchers," and "hepatitis vendors" who give tattoos to minors. But the same forum contained threads about whether or not to shave a body part that has been "inked" (yes, shave it for best effect), the pros and cons of tattooing feet, and one member's link to his private gallery of pornographic, misogynistic tattoos. The question is whether or not teen observers and participants can sort these threads into the sane and the insane, the reasonable and the unreasonable, and the advice that is legitimately helpful and that which is self-destructive.

Teens who fall prey to the modern plagues of adolescence—eating disorders, self-injury, illegal drugs, and the like—now have unimaginable resources at their fingertips. They can join support groups for the anorexic "lifestyle," they can consult how-to sites on cutting and other forms of self-injury, and they can look up formulas for prescription drug cocktails. On a community "pro-anorexia" blog I found the following entry:

> I want the fabric of my coat to drape over my shoulders, I want my collar bones
> to be apparent. . . . I want my dress to not be able to stay on my body. I want to
> appear delicate . . . weak . . . only I will know just how strong I am.

In other entries on this blog, participants post lists of the foods they have eaten that day and ask questions about one another's dieting and fasting techniques. Does the one-bagel-a-day diet work? Is water-fasting unsafe? Where do you get Dextrim and how much does it cost? Will you be my Ana (anorexia) buddy? Without the Internet, such support and validation would be much more difficult to come by. Worst of all, parents, other knowledgeable adults, and friends face difficult odds in the face of such a formidable, omnipresent influence as an Internet-based community.

Hatemongering

The Internet is a great public square. The values that inspired its creation do not discriminate among belief systems. As a result, bigots have the same place at the table as those who work for social justice. Perhaps the most troubling by-product of the Internet era has been the new lease on life it has given to extremist hate groups. While ethnic hatred and racism have always been with us, extremists once had to go to great lengths to find one another and organize their efforts. They have now found both community and platform through the Internet, with teens as a particular target audience. Kindred spirits are a click away, and calls to action are easy to instigate. Compare yesterday's laborious distribution of racist leaflets on a few college campuses to today's Internet-enabled delivery. Extremists create professional-looking sites that are hard to discern from those of reputable organizations. With web development tools and adequate funding, their sites look as legitimate as any mainstream organization's efforts.

In its 2003 annual review of hate activity in the United States, the Southern Poverty Law Center (SPLC) identified 497 active hate websites (*Intelligence Report* 2004). The SPLC breaks these sites into several categories: Ku Klux Klan (124), neo-Nazi (73), racist skinhead (23), Christian Identity (29), Black separatist (12), neo-Confederate (24), and the huge category of "other" (212), which includes sites as disparate as Aryan Wear (http://www.aryanwear.com) and the

Westboro Baptist Church (http://www.godhatesfags.com). The fortunes of these groups ebb and flow, and tracking their online identities is a daunting task. Some of the largest and most established organizations, such as the National Alliance, are currently in decline due to changes in leadership. Other umbrella groups and movements, such as the Ku Klux Klan and neo-Nazi groups, are experiencing a resurgence. All have benefited by having a presence on the Internet.

Although it is startling to see the free-speech blue ribbons that adorn hate sites, they serve as reminders that the Constitution protects most speech, even speech that is offensive and debasing. Consider this example. The American White Knights of the Ku Klux Klan supports a site called removejews.com, which features photographs of concentration camp scenes, or "proven ways to remove Jews." A picture of a pile of corpses is captioned "Good Jews"; a picture of the ovens adjoining the gas chambers says "Jew ovens—got any ketchup?" In the United States, such content is legal. Only speech that is libelous, threatens individuals, or persistently harasses specific persons is prohibited (Anti-Defamation League). Regulating the protected speech of racists would require regulating everyone's speech. In today's environment, this approach is neither technically feasible nor morally desirable.

ESPECIALLY FOR TEENS: MUSIC AS MESSAGE

Music is so important in teenage life that its potential as a tool of persuasion warrants separate discussion. While we do not (yet) see concrete evidence that online hate *speech* has made significant strides in recruiting teens to extremist organizations, hate-based *music* might be another story. Music imprints our coming-of-age process with an indelible time stamp, differentiating each generation from the previous one. Those who understand this phenomenon have learned to manipulate it to their advantage. The teen demographic makes up a substantial proportion of the white power music fan base. "Hatecore" artists perform in popular genres like punk, electronic, and rap. Marketing focuses on teens, who are thought to represent the future of the white power movement. Because standard music outlets like retail stores and chains do not carry these products, they are sold online, where teenagers hang out.

White power music is enjoying an unprecedented level of success. Resistance Records, the online commercial music sales arm of the National Alliance, pulled in an estimated $1.3 million annually prior to the 2002 death of leader William Pierce (VH1 News Special 2002). Its website (http://www.resistance.com) has the usual bells and whistles that appeal to teens—a searchable database of artists and titles, music clips to download, and online ordering. But there is much more to be seen. Viewers can access a web board that has an active Resistance Youth group, collections of "Angry White Mail," creatively illustrated "Moron Mail," a "Resistance Radio" link, and "White Wire News." Promotional material for the fan publication *Resistance Magazine* advises readers to "buy in bulk and distribute them to local kids or get your local music stores to carry it." Since Pierce's death and a subsequent shake-up in the extremist world, other hatecore labels now compete with Resistance Records. Teen fans can now also choose from the likes of Diehard Records, Micetrap Distribution, Panzerfaust Records, Vinland Winds Records, and White Power Warehouse.

Even teens who do not self-identify with extremist values may find themselves enjoying the music. One blogger wrote of being accused of racism:

> I am NOT a nazi or nazi sympathizer because i listen to Skrewdriver or Blue Eyed Devils. I listen to the music for it's instrumental values. Nazi music or not you say? Shut up, you're close minded then. Guitars and bass guitars and drumsets do not have opinions, hence, they are not nazis. They are sounds. And a sound is not opinionated either, it is a noise created by frequencies and vibrations. It takes skill to add these frequencies together to make a good guitar solo, or bass riff. So for the instrumental value, i will like ANY BAND I PLEASE, being a WHITE POWER BAND, a RAP group, or even Good Charlotte if they come out with a decent guitar solo for once.

The writer is naive, not understanding the propagandistic role that music frequently plays and his unwitting complicity in it. In this case, the music cannot be separated from the message.

George Burdi, who started Resistance Records in 1993, edited *Resistance Magazine*, and sang for the band Rahowa (racial holy war), eventually cut his ties to white power groups and subsequently gave an interview to the Southern Poverty Law Center in January 2001. When asked about his current perspective on "white pride," he responded:

> People find meaning for their lives in many different places. Some join Star Trek fan clubs, others join the booster club for their local sports team, and other people become NAFTA [North American Free Trade Agreement] protesters. The white power movement was a way for me to find purpose and meaning in my life. (Southern Poverty Law Center 2001)

Far from high-minded ideology, Burdi's involvement in the white power movement was sparked by little more than the typical teen search for identity. He is not so different from the music fan who was surprised when peers labeled him a racist. Burdi trivializes the implications of his choice by equating it to Star Trek fandom. Unfortunately, grown-up white supremacists are capable of much worse damage than are grown-up Trekkies.

PROPAGANDA TECHNIQUES

Grown-up white supremacists and their ilk recognize the Internet as an effective medium with which to advertise their mission, to persuade, and to recruit. The Internet is not the first medium to be used for propaganda purposes, nor are white supremacists the only group to discover the usefulness of various media types as tools of persuasion. Propaganda techniques apply to all modes of persuasive communication, not just the political. In fact, the same tactics are used by the good guys as well as the bad guys, from mainstream advertisers, nonprofit organizations, government agencies, and political campaigns to hatemongers and terrorist groups. Only the modes of delivery have changed over time, influenced by technology and cultural habit. Broadsides gave way to newspapers, radio, and television in turn. Now the arsenal includes websites, online forums, electronic mailing lists, and even spam.

Contemporary scholars began a serious study of the techniques of persuasion during the twentieth century, as new modes of mass communication blossomed and war in Europe loomed. From 1937 to 1942, the independent Institute for Propaganda Analysis published a series of books and newsletters to help Americans understand the tools of political propaganda. The journalists and social scientists who worked at the institute identified seven basic propaganda devices (*Propaganda Analysis* 1937), and their findings have since been adapted, expanded, and retooled for use in lectures, textbooks, and lessons on critical thinking and the mass media. I will have more to say about the specifics of these techniques in the next chapter.

In the meantime, I will put my own spin on describing several common tactics of persuasion, with an emphasis on how they have been used by hate groups. The strategies are most obvious and egregious when used by extremists. This analysis is by no means comprehensive and is undoubtedly idiosyncratic. My goal is to provide an approach to understanding and deconstructing persuasive speech. This model and others like it can serve as a template for teaching students to conduct their own analyses.

Mimicry

Imitation is the sincerest form of flattery. It can be innocuous, as when novice web designers imitate professionals' design techniques, polish, and tone. But some forms of mimicry are deliberate and insidious. One of the worst types is domain name deception, which occurs when someone grabs the rights to a domain name before the logical owner does. A glaring example is the notorious website called Martin Luther King Jr.: A True Historical Examination (www.martinlutherking.org), which is actually operated by the white supremacist organization Stormfront. (See figure 6-1.) Martinlutherking.org has the professional look of a reputable site, with its rollovers and sleek layout. The site is designed to attract the attention of young readers. It sports a bright blue link across the top of the page that reads "Attention Students: Try Our MLK Pop Quiz," and an invitation at the bottom of the page to

FIGURE 6-1

An example of domain name deception: the website "Martin Luther King, Jr.:
A True Historical Examination" (http://www.martinlutherking.org),
which is operated by the white power group Stormfront.

"Bring the Dream to life in your town! Download flyers to pass out at your school." Pornography sites use similar trickery by buying domain names that are close enough to the real ones that unwitting users go to them in error. An infamous example of this bait-and-switch trick was perpetrated by the creators of white-house.com, surprising those who thought they were accessing the real White House site (http://www.whitehouse.gov).

A less frequently used technique is deliberate impersonation, in which false sites masquerade as real ones. The site at http://www.gatt.org mimics in fine detail the website of the World Trade Organization (http://www.wto.org), though the mimic site is also unrelated to its namesake, the General Agreement on Tariffs and Trade. (See figures 6-2 and 6-3.) The fake site is owned by The Yes Men (http://www.theyesmen.org), two political activists who use unconventional and creative methods to oppose globalization efforts. Clones R Us, a favorite site of mine which is no longer available, pretended to be a commercial site where viewers could order a clone of themselves, a celebrity, or a beloved pet. The extensive

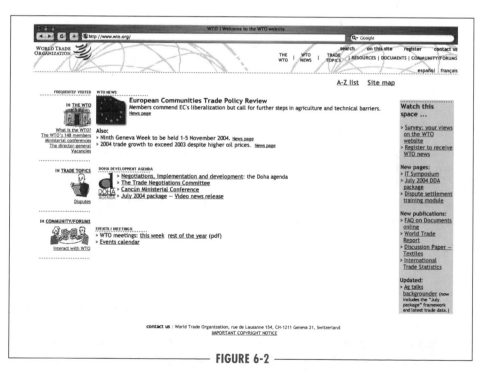

FIGURE 6-2

The legitimate website of the World Trade Organization (http://www.wto.org).

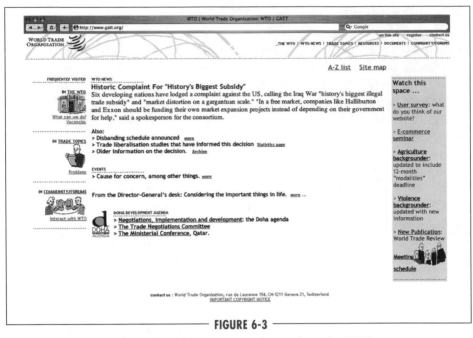

FIGURE 6-3

This website (http://www.gatt.org) mimicking the WTO site
was created by "The Yes Men," two political activists.

price list, the FAQ page, the testimonials, the order forms, and the professional
look made for a convincing commercial website experience. The purpose of the
site was not to deceive, but to stimulate critical thinking about cloning and the
potential consequences of its legalization. Careful readers would eventually find
the small-print disclaimer in the site.

Misuse of Information

Overt trickery is not the only way to deceive. There are as many ways to misuse
information as there are not to. We protect our children, our parents, and our
friends by telling them the truth, but not always the *full* truth. Likewise, content
providers learn to be selective with the information they report. They manipulate
statistics and shape information through creative presentation. The National
Confectioners Association's website tells me what I want to hear about the bene-

fits of chocolate, using reputable scientific documentation (http://www.candyusa
.org/Media/Nutrition/chocolate_goodnews.asp). But it does not tell me what I do
not want to hear about the dangers of overindulgence. The site's information is
absolutely factual, if not entirely complete. As long as there is a grain of truth in
what is being said, the message sounds credible.

Educators reserve most of their concern for more sinister instances of the misuse of information. A lengthy essay titled "Who Rules America?" appears on the
website of the National Alliance (http://www.natall.com/who-rules-america/), a
white power organization. This essay catalogs the ownership of the American mass
media—from electronic news and entertainment media to print newspapers and
magazines—and ties it to Jewish individuals or to those who have "sold out" to
Jews or been "undermined" by Jews. Many of the facts in this story are indis-
putable. The names and companies mentioned are real. The historic role of Jews
in Hollywood and the mass media is no secret, having been celebrated and documented in popular as well as scholarly writing.

But the National Alliance stacks the cards, using this information to draw conclusions that are not warranted by the facts. First, it asserts that the Jewish role
amounts to conspiracy. "Despite a few prominent exceptions, the preponderance
of Jews in the media is so overwhelming that we are obliged to assume that it is
due to more than mere happenstance." Then a call to action is issued:

> But we must not remain silent on this most important of issues! The Jewish con-
> trol of the American mass media is the single most important fact of life, not just
> in America, but in the whole world today. There is nothing—plague, famine, eco-
> nomic collapse, even nuclear war—more dangerous to the future of our people.

It is understood that "our people" are white Christians.

In other cases, statistics are reported out of context, typically without sources,
by those with suspect agendas. Stormfront has done this with crime statistics on its
FAQ page (http://www.stormfront.org/whitenat/white_nationalism_faq.htm):

> For example, on a per-capita basis, Blacks are 49 times more likely to assault a
> White than a White is to assault a Black. Assaults by Whites against Blacks are
> approximately 40 times scarcer than they would be if races were randomly mixed
> and assault rates did not vary by race. The best measure of racism is the number
> of non-economically motivated attacks. Whites score low in this regard, non-
> Whites high.

Where do these numbers come from? What other information might have accompanied them? Stormfront uses the numbers, real or otherwise, to make claims of
reverse discrimination, and concludes that affirmative action policies in the work-

place, college admissions, government contracting, and small business loans all add up to exploitation of the white race.

False Authority

The human psyche seems to crave outside authority, the secure feeling that someone else smarter or better is available as a guide in decision making. Knowing this human tendency, advertisers, propagandists, and others engaged in the business of persuasion often invoke images of such authority. We are all familiar with the television commercials in which a figure dressed in a white lab coat refers to studies that prove the effectiveness of a household cleaner or a mouthwash or some other everyday product. The person in the lab coat is an actor, not a scientist, and the existence of bona fide, externally conducted research is doubtful. Yet these commercials leave a persistent image of authority in the mind of the viewer.

Claims of authority may be misleading, misapplied, or outright false. Professor Arthur Butz of Northwestern University in Illinois uses his personal university web space for expressing his Holocaust revisionist views (http://pubweb .nwu.edu/~abutz/di/intro.html). Although he teaches at a prestigious institution, his field is electrical engineering, not history. He capitalizes on his title and the academic freedom afforded by Northwestern University to espouse beliefs that are based on prejudice and poor scholarship.

Another common strategy is to justify one's position by claiming it emanates from a *higher* authority, typically in the guise of government or religion. Detractors do not wish to appear as though they are arguing against God or country. The discourse of white supremacists often includes religious vocabulary and references. A search engine query on the phrase "white Christian" brings up screen after screen of such examples. The implication, of course, is that a person cannot be a true Christian if he or she is either homosexual or nonwhite. Separatism has suddenly become a prescription from above. Some groups even claim authority from both religion *and* government, as in the Ku Klux Klan slogan "For God, Race, and Country."

The Christian patriot movement is an interesting case of the religion-and-government argument. Ironically, the movement's adherents are neither supporters of the contemporary United States government nor of mainstream Christianity. Sociologist James Aho (1990), who spent two years in northern Idaho studying the movement, noted that Christian patriots distinguish between Law and legality, Morality and legalese. They acknowledge only the "organic Constitution" (the original articles of the Constitution plus the Bill of Rights) and selected edicts from the first five books of the Bible. Therefore, they feel no moral obligation to obey a secular law that is inconsistent with these texts. They get to have it both ways—the blessing of religion and government as well as the freedom to define each to suit a particular worldview. From the Christian patriot perspective, the present United States "Zionist Occupation Government" is biblically and constitutionally illegitimate, bent on promoting non-Christian religions, moral perversion, and equal rights for "unqualified" minorities.

Some groups try to "out-authority" others. Followers of the Christian Identity movement claim preeminent authority by asserting that white, Anglo-Saxon, and Germanic Europeans are descended from the lost tribes of ancient Israel. Contemporary Jews, on the other hand, are descended from an Asian people called the Khazars and are therefore "false Israelites." The most extreme Identity adherents espouse the "two seed" theory in which Jews are the literal seed line of the devil because they are descended from Cain, the unnatural, "mongrel" offspring of Eve and Satan in the guise of the serpent (Ostendorf 2001/2002). (See figure 6-4.) Abel, on the other hand, was the child of Eve and the racially pure Adam. White Christians are therefore an "Adamic" people, the true chosen people of Israel. Jesus was an Aryan, not a Jew.

FIGURE 6-4

Image on the website of the Kingdom Identity Ministries
(http://www.kingidentity.com).

Co-opting Symbols and Traditions

A subtle way to evoke an aura of authority is to adopt the use of established symbols and traditions. Visual imagery and traditional practices are used to convey legitimacy, status, historical imprimatur, and other desirable qualities. It is easy to find examples of symbols that have been adapted by hate groups. American flags and patriotic color schemes adorn the websites of the European-American Unity and Rights Organization (http://www.whitecivilrights.com/), David Duke Online (http://www.duke.org/), and the American Nationalist Union (http://www.anu.org). The National Socialist Movement (http://www.nsm88.com/), which is the American Nazi Party, combines two iconic images—the American flag and the Nazi swastika (which, in turn, is an ancient symbol used by many cultures prior to the Nazis' adoption of it). (See figure 6-5.) Betsy Ross would be astonished to see what has happened to her flag design.

The Anti-Defamation League (ADL) maintains a large visual database of extremist symbols, logos, and tattoos (http://www.adl.org/hate_symbols/default .asp). Each item links to a table of information, which contains the type of group associated with the symbol (e.g., neo-Nazi, racist skinhead), a physical description of the symbol, alternate names, its traditional use and origin, the name of the organization associated with the symbol, and that organization's background and history. Pagan symbols co-opted by extremist groups warrant their own section. Viking insignia and Norse mythological imagery now carry connotations their earlier users would never recognize or understand. Ironically, a number of swastika variants now exist because the traditional symbol, associated with the Nazis, has been banned in many countries.

FIGURE 6-5

The traditions that are co-opted can be as simple as the shared experiences of childhood or common habits of community and family. One of the websites my students find most disturbing is the children's section of the National Alliance online bookstore. Here they see treasured books from their own childhoods co-opted to rep-

The National Socialist Movement combines imagery from the American flag and the Nazi-era swastika to portray the neo-Nazi perspective.

resent "white values" and "white pride." The collection includes standard editions of *Blueberries for Sal, Anne of Green Gables, East o' the Sun and West o' the Moon, Little Men*, and many other familiar titles. My students feel squeamish for sharing the love of these books with people whose values they find reprehensible. They also experience associative culpability, a sense that words and thoughts have been put into their mouths without their permission. The book annotations on the website are particularly damning. Nancy Shaw's 1992 picture book, *Sheep Out to Eat*, in which five hungry sheep wreak havoc in a fancy tea shop, is supposed to tell children to "stick to their own kind." Laura Ingalls Wilder's *Farmer Boy* is described as follows:

> This authentic, fun-filled portrait of farming life in New York state in the 1870s reveals the integrity and values of America's pioneers. It gives a delightful portrayal of White children growing up in a healthy, White environment, learning from their elders, and living in close harmony with the land and all aspects of Nature.

Although Wilder's series has been criticized for its stereotypical depictions of Native Americans (representative of the attitudes of the era), it was hardly written to serve as a model of "a healthy, White environment."

Mainstreaming

The Web allows extremists a medium in which to present themselves as quintessential plain folks, no different from the average American. The viewer sees faces and reads stories that are easy to identify with. The National Alliance (http://www.natall.com/who-is/) tells us that it has

> members from 18 to 92 years old in nearly every walk of life and in a dozen countries. They have an extraordinarily wide variety of backgrounds and skills and interests, but two things they all share are a deep feeling of racial consciousness and a profound sense of personal responsibility.

The site introduces us to a pretty, smiling housewife and mother who claims that all she wants is for her children "to grow up in a clean, healthy, White world, where they won't be a minority." Extremist groups have acquired more mainstream public faces by participating in a broader range of community activities. Many members of the Ku Klux Klan now wear regular street clothes to public functions rather than white robes, and the organization is welcoming more women to the ranks.

Another method of softening an image is to re-coin the vocabulary that is associated with it. Extremists have adopted terms like "racialist" instead of "racist" and "separatism" rather than "supremacy." Racialism is merely the practice of racial "integrity." "Separatism" only signifies respect for the laws of nature, while the term "supremacy" implies control and subjugation, which Stormfront and other groups claim no interest in achieving. This tweaking of vocabulary turns the focus away from hate and places the emphasis on positive qualities like pride, heritage, and self-preservation. In most of this rhetoric, the tone is reasonable rather than strident, calm rather than defensive.

Anti-Mainstreaming

The "plain folks" tactic does not always attract teenagers who, more often than not, want to distance themselves from mainstream society. They already feel different and would rather embrace their status than suffer for it. It does not take long for them to discover that the Internet is a generous host to anyone and anything that is antiestablishment. Anarchists, militia members, cult followers, and peace activists all find a voice in its nonjudgmental bosom. Online, the extreme right meets the extreme left. All manner of strange bedfellows reside side by side, giving alienated teens a huge smorgasbord from which to sample.

Teens are particularly attracted to online resources that have the potential to give their lives a larger and deeper meaning. Teen anarchists can find a home at Anarchist Youth (http://youth.infoshop.org/). Those who are interested in animal rights can sign on with organizations devoted to the excoriation of fast-food chains (e.g., kfccruelty.com). Teens who feel strongly about legitimizing peer-to-peer file sharing will find a community in Downhill Battle (http://www.downhillbattle .org/), an organization devoted to copyright reform and performing artists' rights. On the other side of the political spectrum, teens can take advantage of the many activities available on the National Rifle Association's (http://www.nra.org) youth site. Or they can join National Teens for Life (http://www.nrlc.org/outreach/teens .html), an offshoot of National Right to Life.

Community blogs devoted to causes have also proliferated. On one called "Arrogant not ignorant: Are you a kid with a vision?" I read an entry from an anguished teen who had become a vegetarian and wondered if he was being hypocritical for still wearing his leather boots and jacket. He felt it would be wasteful to discard the items or give them away. Others advised him not to worry:

> If you come across a vegetarian who is offended that you would call yourself one and wear leather, just explain to them how you got the leather before you became one. Say you'd rather wear these back down to dirt than kill the hemp required to weave you a new pair of shoes.

Someone else cautioned him not to be concerned about a potential "pc militant vegan idiot," reflecting a not-unsurprising diversity of opinion within the group.

Despite their engagement in weighty moral issues, teens are still relatively powerless in our society. They reluctantly miss important concerts or protests or activist events because they cannot get permission to skip school or, even more frustrating, cannot find a ride. They rail against world trade, capitalism, and other economic systems that, at some level of consciousness, they realize they benefit from. Activist teens cannot stop being their parents' children. They cannot suddenly become self-supporting, independent beings. Yet their parents' economic support provides them with the wherewithal to protest. They are not necessarily rebels without a cause, but their causes are undermined by their status.

Having anti-mainstream interests does not necessarily signify devotion to lofty humanitarian or political causes. The Internet provides teens with the means to engage in or document unconventional, underground, and even contraband activities. Teens find and exchange information related to rave culture, underground trance/dance clubs, techno music, and popular DJs. There are blog communities that exist solely for the purpose of sharing one's drinking or drugging exploits. At the end of the day, teens are still teens and many are, well, adolescent and rebellious. They throw one another off invitation-only group blogs for infractions like "pissing off the mod" (moderator). They complain in online forums about being required to take standardized tests, being grounded, or being told to make their appearance more conventional. In short, they find sanctuary in the opportunities for expression and community that the Internet bestows.

The new information and communication technologies are here to stay. We would not have it otherwise. But their fallout is undeniable. We cannot afford to sit back and just watch change happen. Our services must adapt, and particularly in the school setting, it is our job to teach teens to meet the challenges of the new environment. Part 3 of this book addresses these next critical steps.

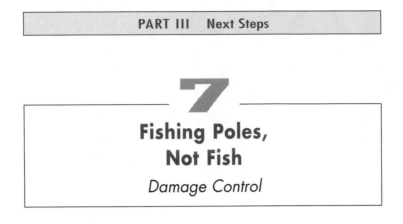

Fishing Poles, Not Fish

Damage Control

When all is said and done, schools and libraries face two basic types of ICT-generated areas of conflict: those that are related to student behavior and those that are related to students' access of inappropriate content. There is some question in my mind about which type actually presents greater difficulties for schools. In our school, behavioral issues—what students do to one another—dominate ICT disciplinary cases. We have not struggled as much with inappropriate content issues. The popular press seems to focus on content problems, which is probably why legislative bodies at all levels regard Internet content filters as the first line of defense in school and library Internet management. One possible explanation for the disparity is that up until recently, many students simply have not had much access to communication technology at school. On the other hand, they *have* had access to information technology. Generally speaking, behavior problems stem from access to communication technology, while inappropriate content problems arise from access to information technology.

Schools employ three basic approaches when dealing with ICT disciplinary issues: regulatory, technological, and pedagogical. The *regulatory* response consists of policies, rules, practices, usage agreements, and other mechanisms that clearly define the acceptable use of ICTs and the consequences for unacceptable use. The *technological* response involves building electronic security fences. These appear in the form of security protection against electronic intrusions and service disruptions, Internet content filters, software that allows teachers to view students' computer screens, and blocks on certain protocols like chat and instant messaging. The *pedagogical* response consists of the variety of methods used to teach students the responsible use of information and communication technologies.

How well do these approaches work? All have their place and each fulfills an important role. Used alone, each method has weaknesses. The drawback of the regulatory approach is that students often forget what they have signed, do not understand it, or do not buy into it. Detection and enforcement are difficult, meaning the consequences may lack backbone. The technological approach is limited because technology fails, students find ways around it, and it requires enormous resources to maintain. Its implementation can also create a false sense of security. For example, the installation of Internet filters sends the message to parents that there are easy, foolproof technological answers to their concerns. The pedagogical approach can also be problematic. Students excel in parroting what teachers want to hear, without necessarily matching their behaviors and beliefs. ICT curricula are relatively new, untested, and labor-intensive. In cases where education and personal responsibility have been emphasized, and rules and security measures minimized, schools have run the risk of losing the integrity of their technology systems (Van Buren 2001).

Some combination of all three strategies—regulatory, technological, and pedagogical—is the commonsense solution. Far from being mutually exclusive, the three approaches can be quite effective in concert. We already know how to implement regulatory and technological solutions. They were our initial lines of defense, so it is relatively easy to find information on policies and acceptable-use documents, on computer security and effective system administration, on filtering software issues, and on school discipline. My main interest lies in integrating the pedagogical approach, in learning how to give students the tools they need to make thoughtful choices and to achieve a deeper understanding of the issues. Because teens use ICTs away from school, in unsupervised, unregulated environments, they need to learn to be their own filters, their own barometers of acceptable and intelligent use of the tools. The rest of this chapter will focus on the pedagogical approach, why it is important, and how it might be accomplished.

LEARNING HOW TO BE: BEHAVIOR

In the early days of the Internet, there were no teachers to tell users how they should behave online. Instead, an ethos developed organically, shaped and refined by the relatively small community of users. This ethos was characterized by self-regulation, the participants preferring internally agreed-upon norms and standards rather than externally imposed authority. Peer pressure was the favored method of encouraging compliance. Today's cyber-communities, much larger and less close-knit than they once were, still formulate codes of conduct and FAQs that prescribe acceptable behaviors. For example, Arlene Rinaldi's well-known guide (http://www.fau.edu/netiquette/net/) outlines behaviors both small-scale and large, from how often to check e-mail to the importance of observing copyright laws when using FTP sites. Rebecca Blood formulated a parallel code for blogging behavior:

> Publish as fact only that which you believe to be true.
>
> If material exists online, link to it when you reference it.
>
> Publicly correct any misinformation.
>
> Write each entry as if it could not be changed; add to, but
>   do not rewrite or delete, any entry.
>
> Disclose any conflict of interest.
>
> Note questionable and biased sources. (2002, 117–21)

When peer pressure fails, the self-regulation ethic can quickly turn aggressive. These are the instances in which enthusiastic netizens use their skills to thwart cyber-miscreants who have committed crimes ranging in gravity from persistent flaming to serious destruction of computer resources. Most of this self-policing activity is fairly informal and spontaneous. For example, users who have misrepresented themselves on discussion boards may be blocked by the site administrator or simply shunned by other users. But some online community policing efforts are highly organized. CyberAngels (http://www.cyberangels.org), an offshoot of the community-based New York City subway-patrolling Guardian Angels, began by hunting pedophiles and software pirates and reporting them to Internet service providers. The organization has now broadened its scope by offering a wide range of education and advocacy services.

The Home Setting

Middle-class teens generally receive their initial training in ICT behavior at home. What does that training look like? A study commissioned by the Girl Scouts of the USA (Girl Scout Research Institute 2002) found that "most advice and rules girls receive about the Internet are in the form of prohibitive statements, rather than proactive advice about real-life situations that occur for them online" (11). Parental advice is very general, usually in the form of directives "not to" (not to give out personal information, not to go to inappropriate websites, and so on). The quantity of this advice subsides once Internet access in the home becomes routine.

The inherent weakness of this strategy is that girls rate themselves as being much more computer-savvy than their parents. They name a number of things they can do online without their parents' knowledge, such as participating in chat room conversations, reading their parents' e-mail, forming romantic attachments, setting up meetings with strangers, and accessing porn sites. At the same time, they feel that they are smart enough not to do things that are truly "bad" or would get them into serious trouble. Girls draw a distinction between what they are not *allowed* to do (which they attribute in part to parental ignorance) and what they themselves believe would be dangerous. They want their parents to acknowledge their experience and common sense. So while 75 percent of the girls have parents who set household rules about Internet use, 57 percent admit to having broken some of those rules (Girl Scout Research Institute 2002).

In part, this deception occurs because girls feel that their parents are concerned about the wrong things. Instead of worrying about their daughters spending too much time online socializing, girls feel that there should be more concern about the kinds of information girls can access if they want to, their online behavior (e.g., lying and cursing), the unsavory people they can meet online, and practical matters, such as invasions from hackers and viruses. The report is careful to note that although girls often act with a maturity that is well beyond their years, they are still young and vulnerable. Bad things do happen, girls do make poor choices, and their common sense does not always prevail in complex situations.

The report urges adults to provide proactive rather than reactive advice. Girls are less likely to confide in their parents about bad things that happen online if they think they will get in trouble. Similar advice could be given to parents about their children's online game playing. If parents take the time to become familiar with the games and with their children's involvement in them, their dictates will carry more weight. If parents simply say no, kids will go underground with their game playing or their questionable behavior. Parents need to create an environment that is both realistic and protective.

The School Setting

When it started becoming obvious that the Internet was in schools to stay, educators realized they needed to do something about managing its implementation. Kids had already found all sorts of ways to get into trouble online. Most of them had not benefited from the mentoring of Internet old-timers, who could have passed on their self-regulatory spirit and sense of obligation to the expanding community of web users. Some educators made the mistake of responding to these early problems by placing draconian limitations on in-school Internet use, rendering its presence fairly meaningless. Others learned hard lessons about what can happen in the absence of policies and programs delineating appropriate use.

The high-tech school that Van Buren (2001) studied for three years is an interesting case of what happens when a culture of trust, rather than regulation, is fostered. She discovered the existence of an informal, student-taught hacker curriculum which she believes is common to many schools but is generally invisible to teachers and administrators. Students who are "enrolled" in these academies enjoy a sense of superiority over other students and over the adults who are ostensibly in charge. Van Buren learned that the disciplinary system held different lessons for the less computer-proficient students than for the high-proficiency students, who were able to cover their tracks. Low-proficiency students were more likely to get caught when they broke rules and so were punished at disproportionate levels. At the same time, they were more inclined to abide by the school's culture of trust than were their high-proficiency peers. The lesson? The virtual locks and other security devices at this school only served to keep the honest students honest. The real "criminals" had no trouble disabling them, resulting in the loss of substantial staff and student time spent dealing with the effects of student misuse and abuse of the school network.

Still, it is hard to know what course to follow. Computer-savvy students are quite sensitive to preemptive security measures that they view as punitive or patronizing. Van Buren observes that the use of Internet content filters communicates to students that they cannot be trusted, and that they ultimately are not capable of learning to use computers responsibly. She notes that "such measures also represent an irresistible challenge for hacker students who view network restrictions imposed by school officials as an opportunity to demonstrate their hacking prowess to their peer group while simultaneously subverting institutional authority" (56–57). This assessment certainly rings true when I think about my own school environment. The installation of filtering software would be tantamount to issuing an "I dare you" challenge to break and enter.

Technology writer Steven Levy (2003) believes that putting the kibosh on online activities is a recipe for disaster and that, in fact, computers and online access are essential tools for survival in today's society. Yes, kids need protection from the seedy side of technology. But they have a right to computers, web access, and "wise, wired teachers" who can keep in touch with students and parents online and who understand the difference between multimedia glitz and real learning opportunities (S. Levy 2003, E30). Students respond to genuine demonstrations of respect and a consistent approach to technology management. While computer-savvy students may have hacker inclinations, Van Buren observed that whether a student moves toward "white hat" hacking or "black hat" cracking depends on the school climate. Key indicators of this climate are the ways in which ethical online behavior is modeled by the school's computer-related curriculum and its policies and procedures. The litmus test of success lies in the balance that a school manages between maintaining network security and protecting students' online civil liberties.

TEACHING APPROACHES

How is ICT ethics training best accomplished? Though its particular application to technology is new, ethics education itself has a long history. Though labeled variously over time (e.g., citizenship training, character development, values education), it always attempts to influence moral growth and development through the formal education process.

As described in chapter 5, contemporary approaches to ethics education have been heavily influenced by the work of sociologist Émile Durkheim (1925/1961), psychologist Jean Piaget (1932), and, perhaps most importantly, psychologist Lawrence Kohlberg (1958, 1984). In Durkheim's view, the purpose of moral education is to teach adherence to societal norms via the transmission of traditions, using stories and examples and modeling desired behaviors. Through this behavioral psychology approach, students feel part of the larger society and have respect for its rules and symbols of authority. Piaget's position is that children should be placed in situations which require them to actively struggle with issues of fairness, ultimately choosing for themselves what is moral. Through this cognitive psychology approach, learners develop a deep understanding of societal values and a sense of ownership in them. Kohlberg expanded Piaget's stages of moral development and created an assessment technique using fictional moral dilemmas. The influence of Piaget and Kohlberg is seen in contemporary dialogue-centered curricula.

Early on in the growth of the Internet, educators dipped into their toolkits and began to develop ICT ethics education programs that reflect the influence of these theoretical traditions. A very useful guide for schools was published in 1992 by the National Institute of Justice (Sivin and Bialo). Although 1992 is now considered ancient history in the life span of the Internet, the advice given in this slim monograph is still surprisingly fresh and relevant. Schools are counseled to take action on two fronts by (1) setting consistent school policies that model how students should behave, and (2) incorporating technology ethics education into the curriculum.

I believe that the choice of the term "model" is an important one in this context. The Durkheim perspective tells us that it is not enough for schools to simply dictate rules and regulations. School personnel must practice what they preach by purchasing legal copies of software, abiding by fair-use guidelines, using good netiquette, observing online privacy rights, and otherwise respecting community standards. If they do not, they will have created a "Do what I say, not what I do" milieu, which is a recipe for disaster where computer-savvy students are concerned. High standards of staff behavior are easy to mandate, but tricky to realize. The teachers who are not comfortable with technology will not know enough about what they are doing to model appropriately or effectively. And the teachers who are ineffective role models in nontechnological matters are unlikely to take up the mantle when it comes to technology.

When it comes to the curriculum component, the 1992 guide suggests that information technology systems be presented as extensions and reflections of human society. ICTs are created by people and used by people. Therefore, like other human-engineered artifacts, they can be used in a variety of ways—productively or unproductively, to help or to hurt. Echoing Kohlbergian thinking, the guide's authors stress that behaving with moral responsibility, no matter what the context, is ultimately each student's individual choice to make.

Since 1992, guides for the formal teaching of ICT ethical concepts have become widely available. Nancy Willard's *Computer Ethics, Etiquette, and Safety for the 21st-Century Student* is a text for students in grades six through twelve published by the International Society for Technology in Education. Each item in the table of contents can be used as a discussion starter, with topics such as "Those are real people out there," "Keep it private," "Watch where you are looking," "Credit the source," and "Do your part" (Willard 2002, vii–viii). Another useful example is Doug Johnson's *Learning Right from Wrong in the Digital Age* (2003). Both books contain exercises and activities that are appropriate for classroom use.

An ethics curriculum can be taught formally or informally. As a formal curriculum, ethics is the subject of explicit units of study. An informal curriculum generally occurs more spontaneously, at points of need, when a teacher or librarian seizes a moment of relevance in the context of other activities or studies. An informal curriculum is also a by-product of the consistent cross-curricular implementation of policy, of modeling desired behaviors. For example, an implicit lesson is transmitted when teachers in multiple academic departments present the same expectations for citing online sources. Individual teachers may teach the different citation styles that are appropriate to their disciplines, but they speak in one voice when it comes to basic messages regarding plagiarism and the obligation to give credit where credit is due.

ORGANIZED PROGRAMMING: THE TRACK RECORD

The jury is still out regarding students' response to an overt ethics curriculum. Existing character education programs have met with mixed success. One of the best known of these is the Drug Abuse Resistance Education (DARE) program, which is still widely in use. However, long-term studies now show that DARE graduates are just as likely to use drugs as young people who have not been through the program (Kanoff 2003). Parallel educational efforts are under way to promote sexual abstinence before marriage. Title V, a program of the 1996 welfare reform act, mandated that considerable federal funds be used toward the implementation of such programs. More varied than the DARE curriculum, these programs are harder to evaluate as a whole. Many incorporate abstinence pledges, in which teens (usually in some sort of public ceremony) sign pledges that they will remain sexually abstinent until marriage. Researchers have found that two outcomes are likely: (1) teens alter their definition of sex to exclude anything but actual intercourse, believing that oral sex is not actually "having sex," and (2) when they do break their pledges, they are less likely to use protection such as condoms (*Christian Century* 2003).

The "just say no" approach of these values education programs reflects the Durkheim behaviorist tradition, in which the child is seen as an empty vessel waiting to be filled with the right kind of knowledge. But simply telling teens and preteens what is right and what is wrong has not proven effective in the long term, even with the attractive incentives that are built into programs like DARE. After all, the society at large models behavior that contradicts the messages of these programs. Kohlberg-influenced educators, on the other hand, have favored Socratic approaches infused with opportunities for dialogue. Examples of these can be found in the curricula used by International Baccalaureate programs (Hamelink 2000) or in the hypothetical scenario method advocated by the National Institute of Justice guide (Sivin and Bialo 1992). At my school, we use a dilemma discussion approach that is similar to Socratic dialogue, but sets the "moral of the story" in a context which is relevant to a teen's experience and, we hope, generates deeper engagement. Excerpts from some of these discussions appear in chapter 5. Most of the scenarios we use are based on real situations that have occurred at school. Here is one example:

> Jules has walked away from a lab computer without logging off. Trish sits down and, still logged in as Jules, sends inflammatory e-mail messages out to a number of students and posts similar messages on the class newsgroup.

The students first discuss this scenario in an online forum. The technology director and I then follow up with an in-class discussion, during which we tell the story of the real event (without using real names!) that inspired the scenario. In this example, a particularly hateful message was sent to the all-student mailing list, seemingly from one student, in which another student was spoken about in obscene terms. This instance of impersonation and slander caused the school to institute new procedures. Messages that are sent to the all-school e-mail lists now go to the technology director first. He screens them for such criteria as obscenity and defamation of character. Students are well aware of this policy because message headers sent to the all-school lists are all tagged "by way of" the technology director. During this class discussion, we clarify that regular (non-mailing list) e-mail messages are *not* routinely screened. In fact, students learn that the technology director is actually prohibited from reading personal mail unless the school principal suspects foul play and directs an investigation. Furthermore, we tell students that nothing prevents individuals from creating their own all-school mailing lists, which would then bypass the technology director.

Telling such tales in class serves several purposes. First, students learn that infractions of system rules can hurt real people, and that access to ICTs is at once a powerful and fragile privilege. Second, processes are demystified. As students come to understand the technology director's role and certain practical issues (e.g., the extremely high level of e-mail traffic—more than any human being could monitor), they realize their e-mail is relatively free from administrative snooping. Third, students learn that their school is not infallible, and that the adults in charge have also had hard lessons to learn. What's more, their teachers trust them enough to confide these weaknesses and, even more astonishing, tell them how to get around the system if they wish. Finally, they learn that their teachers have students' best interests at heart.

It is extremely difficult, however, to evaluate the success of dialogue-based programs like ours. I have often wondered if our students are "nicer" as a result of our particular efforts. When I am inclined to think so, I have only to remember the student who, after he was caught in an act of transgression, wondered if he was going to be the subject of our next ethical scenario. He knew exactly what he had done wrong and why it was wrong. He even knew how his actions fit into our curriculum. But his awareness did not change his behavior.

LEARNING HOW TO SEE: CONTENT

In pre-Internet days, becoming a published author was something of a production. An outside entity—a book publisher, a magazine editor, an editorial board, some kind of organization—had to vet the content before it saw the light of day. Now, with minimal effort and resources, anyone can "publish" on the Web. Consumers of all ages need to be aware and to *beware*, recognizing that not everything they see online is what it appears to be. And much as we would like, there is no simple formula for discerning good web content from bad. At one time, teachers rather routinely forbade .com resources on student bibliographies. The theory was that any information that did not originate from a .edu site or, just possibly, a .org site, was highly suspect. We have since learned that such coarse methods of content evaluation are not very meaningful. But some level of guidance must be provided to students if they are to make intelligent use of the Web.

Identifying Evaluation Criteria

What standards should be used to evaluate online content? Typical school evaluation rubrics emphasize academic criteria. Students are prompted to look for evidence of authority, currency, documentation, and bias. But evaluation criteria must be flexible enough to accommodate a broad definition of information and a wide range of information providers, from hobbyists and geeks to nonprofit organizations and commercial interests. In my own evaluation checklist, I have added advocacy and enthusiasts' sites, as well as the all-forgiving category of "other" which allows students to simply explain what they see. Students are then better equipped to evaluate advocacy sites like the Republican National Committee (http://www.rnc.org/), the League of American Bicyclists (http://www.bikeleague .org/), or even the International Federation of Competitive Eating (http://www .ifoce.com). They know how to approach collaborative fiction-writing sites or movie-reviewing sites. There are vast qualitative differences among resources like these, yet the standard-issue academic evaluation rubrics do not fit them.

Not only is the distinction between academic and nonacademic content blurring, but "credible" and "authoritative" are even becoming relative terms. How does one classify a news and commentary-style blog written by a public personality? Is it ever appropriate to cite one for a school research paper? Teenager Qingshuo Wang (2003), who wrote an article for *Voice of Youth Advocates* on the journalistic function of blogs, posed some intriguing questions: "How do we find the blogs of the real September 11 witnesses? Which blogs are providing credible news? And which blogs are actually useful news as opposed to personal mumbling?" (28) He calls these sorts of blogs excellent complements to traditional journalism because they contain rich personal depictions of events and act as checks to the biases of mainstream media. Some can be regarded as authoritative, some cannot. The reader must evaluate them in terms of his or her own individual information needs and interests.

As educators, we need to ask ourselves about the scope of our lessons. There are increasingly compelling reasons to include quasi-academic and nonacademic web resources in evaluation lessons. Teaching kids "out-of-school" content promotes lifelong learning, which has long been a goal of mainstream education. Perhaps the most compelling rationale for broadening our scope is that teens typically use the Internet much more at home than they do at school (NetDay 2004). At home, teens enjoy more time online, endure less supervision, and are limited by fewer restrictions. Most of all, kids hang out online, so it makes sense to meet them on their own terms, or at least their own territory, with lessons that will help them stay safe and put them in control rather than under control. Here are some examples of the way such lessons could look:

> Students critique and compare music-reviewing sites. They look for evidence of professionalism and conflict of interest.
>
> Students compare and contrast different online financial services, tracking the stock market advice given by each. Or students evaluate differences in how these services profile individual companies, then compare this information to the companies' own online promotional material.
>
> Students find auction sites in addition to large ones like eBay and analyze the differences between them. They conduct price and service comparisons across sites, as well as with standard online retail outlets.
>
> Students compare the information on a disease in different types of sources: consumer-oriented websites, websites designed for medical professionals, and web boards or newsgroup postings.
>
> Students follow the same news story as it is covered by different media outlets, including blogs.

Evaluating Websites

I would like to think we are beyond the days when teens believed everything they read online. Technology guru Alan November (1998) once told the story of a four-teen-year-old boy who found Arthur Butz's Holocaust denial site and, because it was hosted by Northwestern University, assumed it contained credible, interesting new information. This boy was not only naive about the wide manner of information that can be published on the Web, he also lacked the critical evaluation skills to properly interpret the information he saw. Today's fourteen-year-olds, who generally have had more exposure to questionable web content—at least enough to know it exists—are still unlikely to be very sophisticated about deconstructing it. There is much to be said for purposely taking students to a site such as Butz's and, as a collaborative activity, working through its pitfalls using standard media analysis criteria. This exposure serves as a kind of preemptive inoculation.

Though hate sites are but one piece in the panoply of questionable web content, they grab teens' attention—so much so that I have found it useful to center some of my lessons around them. When I show my students the martinluther king.org site, they respond as one would expect. All of them are appalled, and distressed that racism could be expressed in such an overt, public manner. Once the fact of the site is absorbed, though, there is (at least initially) not too much more to say except "How awful!" The real learning seems to occur a bit later when I display websites that *unwittingly* link to martinlutherking.org.

Unfortunately, such sites are not difficult to find. By using the "who's linking" features of various search engines, or by simply conducting a search on "Martin Luther King" and "Historical Examination," the sites are easy to pick out. Authors of the sites include teachers who are creating class websites on King, broadcast outlets commemorating the King holiday, students writing term papers, activist organizations providing information on King's life, and even public libraries posting resource pages on King. By not properly examining martinlutherking.org before linking to it, each of these website authors is guilty of perpetuating its message. Their lack of care makes a great impression on my students because it is palpable proof of what happens in the absence of evaluation.

On the other hand, some care must be taken in the selection of websites to analyze in the school setting. Scenes of wartime atrocities, especially when they are being used for propaganda purposes by one side or another, are obvious fodder for deconstruction lessons. However, such depictions may be unsuitable for school-aged children. Between the May 11, 2004, release of the videotaped beheading of American hostage Nicholas Berg in Iraq and a May 23 story on National Public Radio's *All Things Considered*, at least half a dozen high school teachers around the country were suspended for showing their students the video or allowing them to download it in school (Sanchez 2004).

Media outlets struggle with the problem of appropriateness on a somewhat different level. They may be accused of merely promoting propagandists' efforts by publishing or broadcasting such material. Teachers must ask themselves the same question and, in addition, be concerned about the developmental readiness of their students to assimilate the lessons of such exposure. Are there some materials that are inappropriate for school in all cases? Are such lessons worth the potential costs? Or can the point be made in other ways?

Local sensibilities must be respected when considering the use of sensitive materials. Otherwise, lessons may produce unintended, undesirable consequences. A school librarian once told me that she could never present the National Alliance website's anti-Semitic rhetoric in class because it might simply reinforce existing stereotypes in her multiracial school population. In her situation, deconstruction lessons would probably have to begin with more neutral material, then progress to stronger examples as students' evaluation skills and sensitivities grew in sophistication. Conducting analyses away from computers might also be in order. Guided discussion could then focus on an uncluttered paragraph of text, without the distractions of keyboards and screens. No matter what the situation, the approach must be flexible: it must be sensitive to the local setting, the nature of the material, and, above all, the best interests of the students.

Developing Critical Evaluation Skills

When it comes to being able to deal with questionable Internet content, information evaluation skills are the first line of defense. After the initial shock of exposure to sites such as martinlutherking.org, the next step is to systematize the viewing with analytical techniques like discourse analysis. Basic propaganda devices are time-honored and well-worn, yet their deconstruction must be relearned by each new generation. Even young teens are capable of conducting such exercises. As long ago as 1938, the Institute for Propaganda Analysis was developing instructional materials for schools. Consider the following exercises, excerpted from the institute's *Propaganda: How to Recognize It and Deal with It,* in terms of their relevancy to analyzing material found on the Web:

> Find examples of lack of precision in speech, such as "This is the greatest nation in the world," or "The Japanese are an inferior race." Ask: What do these statements mean? What are these particular claims asserting?

> Test authorities cited in commercial and political propagandas by asking: (1) Is the authority scientific in his methods; that is, does he begin with hypotheses which he holds only as hypotheses until they are documented by research—facts, figures, statistics; (2) Does the authority have any important self-interest at stake? (3) Are you accepting the authority simply because he is a fashionable authority; if so *why* is he fashionable? Does the reason in any way impair his authoritativeness?

> Make a scrapbook list of popular beliefs based on lack of evidence. These beliefs may be economic, social, or racial. Make a corresponding list of superstitions which still exist, of superstitions which existed a century ago—for example, the New England belief in witchcraft. (*Propaganda* 1938, 54–55)

Some basic questions must be asked when evaluating information found on the Web. What is the purpose of the website? What is its authorship? What clues, technical and otherwise, reveal this information? And what devices are being used to persuade readers, or even deceive them?

PURPOSE

There are really two facets to the notion of purpose (in any information context, not just the Web): the purpose of the website itself, and the user's purpose in needing the information. For example, a student who is assigned to write a science paper will need to be able to distinguish between popular science writing and peer-reviewed research literature. There are markers that identify each type, whether the material is found online or in print. If the scholarly literature proves incomprehensible, the student will need to reevaluate her purpose and look for something simpler, or possibly some basic science reference sources to help her decipher the literature.

In assessing the purpose of a website, there are some important questions to ask. Is there an "About Us" section? Do the statements there seem to fit what the viewer sees? Who is the site's intended audience? Is the information original to the site or taken from elsewhere? Is there value-added material? The teen looking for samples of an artist's work might appreciate a site that offers both the art and some explanatory material. Is Information-with-a-capital-I even the point of the site? It may be a discussion area, a collaborative poetry-writing community, or a site that provides services rather than information per se. Students need to cast their evaluation of a site in terms of their own interest in it. Perhaps an advocacy site is desired precisely for the purpose of articulating a specific point of view. Or a blog may be useful as a primary source, when a student needs the perspective of someone who has witnessed important events or represents a certain perspective.

AUTHORSHIP

Another critical key to understanding the purpose of a website lies in clarifying its authorship. Once authorship is clear, purpose often becomes evident. In the online world, standard identifiers, like a book's title page or an article byline, either may not exist or may appear in unexpected places and guises. The search process itself can mask authorship. For example, keyword searches in an online catalog produce bibliographic records that prominently display title and author fields. By contrast, keyword searches in a search engine can land the searcher smack in the middle of a website, without clear reference to its "front" page. This result is like having a catalog search send the user directly to page 157 of a book, with no direct reference to title, author, or table of contents.

Certain problems of authorship, such as conflict of interest and bias, are perennial concerns. For example, through deceptive reporting practices, William Randolph Hearst's newspapers were able to stir up public sentiment to such a degree that they actually helped start the Spanish-American War of 1898—all for the purpose of selling more newspapers. In pre-Internet days, students were taught to spot editorial perspective and analyze argumentation techniques. Such lessons continue to be relevant, regardless of the format of publication. In the context of the Web, many of the telltale signs of conflict of interest can be taught. Who is the author affiliated with? Does the author benefit in some way from the information on the website? Is something for sale? At the site of Nicotine Free Kids (http://nicotinefreekids.com), readers will find quitting tips, tobacco facts, lesson plans for educators, and information about exercise, weight gain, and stress. However, the company that supports the site also markets a smoking cessation program. All links eventually lead to the pages on which this product can be purchased. The information and the program itself may be valuable, but must be weighed in the context of this inherent conflict.

Practice can make perfect, or at least much better. The simple process of writing a bibliography entry helps students understand what they are looking at. Bibliography-generation software like NoodleBib (http://www.noodletools.com/) enhances learning because it prompts the user with questions for each entry, first about the source type, and then about each bibliographic element within the source. Another technique is to create "Whodunit" assignments, in which students determine the authorship and purpose of various websites. My version of this activity can be found at http://www.uni.uiuc.edu/library/computerlit/sourcing.html. One site favored by librarians for this exercise is titled "The True but Little Known Facts about Women and Aids" (http://147.129.226.1/library/research/AIDSFACTS.htm). Authored by a Dr. Juatta Lyon Feuel from the University of Santa Anita, it contains a list of works "sited" and touts facts such as: "The Atlantic Center for Disease Control recently confirmed that no woman who has remained vehicularly exculpatient until the age of at least 53 has ever contracted AIDS." It takes my eighth-grade students several minutes to figure out that the site is a spoof (be sure to say the author's name aloud), and several more to determine that it was developed by John Henderson, a librarian at Ithaca College, for the purpose of teaching website evaluation.

Librarians can teach simple technical tricks that help students determine authorship. One technique is to just shorten the URL of a site when there is no built-in navigation to its true home. When authorship proves more elusive, a visit to Network Solutions (http://www.networksolutions.com), the largest registrar of domain names, is the next step. By clicking on their "whois" link, I was able to discover who is behind the site that spoofs the real World Trade Organization site (http://www.gatt.org), discussed in chapter 6. (See figure 7-1.) From there, I went to the source (theyesmen.org) to find out more about their mission. I cast the net even wider by checking the URLs of the domain servers (rtmark.com and ns2.plagiarist.org), learning more than I ever dreamed it was possible to know about the machinations of The Yes Men and their associates. I used the same strategy to find out that the hate group Stormfront is responsible for the martinlutherking.org site.

DECONSTRUCTION TECHNIQUES

Fortunately, educators do not have to reinvent the wheel when it comes to teaching students how to spot the rhetorical tricks described in chapter 6. Most "point

```
WHOIS RECORD FOR

gatt.org                          Back-order this name

                                  Make an Offer for this name

Registrant:
Bichlbaum, Andy (HAYTIWGYUD)
553 167th Ave.
Glendale Park, NY 12201
US

Domain Name: GATT.ORG

Administrative Contact, Technical Contact:
Bichlbaum, Andy (GDSKCEYELI) andrew@theyesmen.org
553 167th Ave.
Glendale Park, NY 12201
US
213-592-3813

Record expires on 30-Oct-2005.
Record created on 03-Aug-2002.
Database last updated on 3-Jun-2004 15:16:34 EDT.

Domain servers in listed order:

RTMARK.COM 64.115.210.58
NS2.PLAGIARIST.ORG 132.239.126.96
```

FIGURE 7-1

A "whois" search reveals the name of the true owner of the WTO-mimic website and provides the URL for the domain server that hosts "The Yes Men" site.

of view" websites can still be evaluated in terms of the seven devices identified by the Institute for Propaganda Analysis (*Propaganda Analysis* 1937): name-calling, glittering generality, transfer, testimonial, plain folks, card stacking, and bandwagon. The first two, name-calling and glittering generality, occur when words are used to link people or ideas to either negative or positive associations. These are loaded terms like "family values," "tax-and-spend-liberal," "redneck," "patriot," "terrorist," "freedom fighter"—and so on. The second two devices, transfer and testimonial, imply false or unwarranted connections to persons, ideas, or symbols that, again, carry certain associations. We see this in the depiction of American flags by hate groups, in first-person testimonials on political party websites, and in celebrity endorsements of consumer products. The plain folks device occurs when speakers claim that they are "just like everyone else," as the hate group National Alliance does in describing its members, who are "from 18 to 92 years old in nearly every walk of life" (http://www.natall.com/who-is/). Card stacking is the technique of piling up arguments, evidence, statistics, and information or misinformation to slant an argument—particularly for the purposes of inciting fear. Conspiracy theorists are especially adept at employing this tool. Finally, the bandwagon device lures us with the argument that "everyone else is buying/ believing/ doing this, so you should be too."

Several watchdog organizations now provide their own guides to understanding online hate. Tolerance.org, a web project of the Southern Poverty Law Center, provides screen shots of four different hate sites and "tours" the viewer through the misstatements on each one (http://www.tolerance.org/hate_internet). The Media Awareness Network, based in Canada, delineates the familiar strategies of hate groups—the use of pseudoscience and intellectualism, historical revisionism, patriotism, misinformation, nationalism, hate symbols, and claims of "racialism" rather than racism (http://www.media-awareness.ca/english/issues/online_hate/ deconst_online_hate.cfm). Lesson plans and classroom activities are also available on this website. The Anti-Defamation League, in addition to its database of hate symbols, provides extensive material on recognizing and combating hate, both on and off-line. For example, "Poisoning the Web: Hatred Online" (http://www.adl .org/poisoning_web/poisoning_toc.asp) documents the growing presence of hate groups online.

These efforts have not gone unnoticed by their targets. David Duke's organization, the European-American Unity and Rights Organization (http://www .whitecivilrights.com/), apparently regards them as enough of a threat to have produced its own counter-material. A section called "Teaching Tolerance" (http:// www.duke.org/teaching_tolerance.html) provides the white supremacist spin on teaching strategies:

> We suggest that teachers should clearly instruct students of the overwhelming European American role in the foundation of the United States of America, and of their cultural and scientific contributions that have benefited all races. Such teaching would reduce alienation among White students and lessen resentment among minorities toward White students and teachers.

The site also contains several diatribes against the Anti-Defamation League, asking on its front page, "Who watches the so-called Watch Dog groups?" In reference to teachers, it cautions:

> They should especially be aware of material from the ADL (Anti-Defamation League of B'nai B'rith—a Jewish supremacist organization). ADL material promotes minority resentment and hostility against White Christians, as well as self-guilt among young White students.

A side-by-side comparison of this text with text from the ADL site would make an interesting exercise. The term *supremacist* is used by both sides. Whose definition stands?

Deconstruction techniques can also be taken home. I have found it particularly productive to have students analyze a set of purportedly educational websites for their parents after we have finished our in-class practice. (See exercise 7-1.)

EXERCISE 7-1

EVALUATING WEBSITES: SHARING THE FUN

Take your parent(s)/guardian(s) on a tour of the websites you visited at http://www.uni.uiuc.edu/library/computerlit/evaluatingsites.html. Show them the high points *and* the low points. See if they can spot the tricks!

If you don't have Web access at home, see me and we'll figure out an alternative.

To get full credit, signed forms (below) are due by _____.

Dear parents/guardians,

As a parent myself, I know how difficult it can be to get students to share their school day experiences. In the case of this particular assignment, I have a special interest in involving you. First, I'd like you to know what is happening in this Computer Literacy 1 unit on web searching and website evaluation. As you know, there is a lot of questionable material on the Internet and we want our students to be critical consumers. Second, I feel strongly that parents and teachers are in this effort together. Your involvement is key to helping students understand the importance of being informed users of electronic (and paper!) information sources.

Please be aware that one site on this list is highly offensive. It is included so students learn to look beyond surface credentials and institutional affiliation. If you have any questions or concerns, please do not hesitate to contact me.

Thanks very much,
Frances Jacobson Harris
University Laboratory High School Librarian

My son/daughter _____ took me on a tour of the websites found at http://www.uni.uiuc.edu/library/computerlit/evaluatingsites.html. He/she helped me understand how to evaluate the sites for accuracy, objectivity, and authority.

Parent/Guardian signature _____ Date _____

Comments (optional):

This assignment requires that students not only understand what they have seen online but understand it at a deep enough level to be able to articulate their knowledge to others. It brings parents into the fold, keeping them informed as well as involving them in the learning process. Students have a chance to model what they know and to display their competence. Finally, the activity gives the family a set of information evaluation tools to use in the future.

What comes next? Put students more directly in the driver's seat. Applying evaluation principles to genuine information needs will give meaning to students' abstract knowledge. Students can be asked to develop evaluation rubrics to suit their own individual tasks and projects. They, rather than their librarians, can create research pathfinders (source-finding "maps") or annotated bibliographies that are meaningful to the context in which they are working. Outside school, they will be prepared to develop criteria that are appropriate to more personal information needs. The goal is to make thinking about evaluation automatic, a habit of mind that is deeply ingrained into the process of information use in any context.

Putting It
All Together

A s the new generation flocks to the Internet without a backward glance, libraries may begin to look like relics from another age. At the same time, librarians are becoming deeply aware of how much their services are needed. The important teaching and learning processes discussed in the previous chapter do not happen by magic. "The Digital Disconnect" (Levin and Arafeh 2002), a Pew Internet and American Life Project report, tells us that students employ five metaphors when explaining how they use the Internet for school: as virtual text-book and reference library; tutor and study shortcut; study group; guidance coun-selor; and locker, backpack, and notebook. If these metaphors are taken literally by the right (or wrong) people, then a number of us—librarians and school coun-selors, at the least—will soon be out of jobs. But the data, perhaps unintentionally, also reveals a number of misconceptions these students have about information searching, scholarship, and the nature of information found online. While teens think they are getting everything they need online, they are missing out in critical ways. Neither the Pew researchers nor the teens they studied seemed to grasp the significance of these deficits.

In her critique of "The Digital Disconnect," Joyce Valenza (2004) discusses the importance of asking the right questions. She points out that the report tells us much that we already know about teens and the Internet. Yes, teens generally prefer to use the Internet for research and homework. They feel that they know more about the Internet than their teachers do. They are disappointed that teachers do not more fully exploit the Internet's possibilities in the classroom and are frustrated by restricted access at school. The teens who were studied were selected for being "Internet savvy," but the researchers seemed to equate time spent online with expertise. The questions they asked tell us *what* services teens use on the Internet, but not much about *how* teens use those services. In other words, the study stops short of assessing what librarians value most—the students' level of information literacy. Nevertheless, the fact that teens *think* they know all they need to know is an important factor in how we plan our services and programs.

INFORMATION STRUCTURES AND INFORMATION MEANINGS

"Format agnostic" is the label Abram and Luther (2004) ascribe to this younger generation. Because web search results can include anything from websites and blogs to encyclopedia and magazine articles, teenagers do not think in terms of source type:

> Information is information, and NextGens see little difference in credibility or entertainment value between print and media formats. Their opinions can be modified and influenced by an information ocean that does not differentiate between journals and books, network or cable television, or blogs or web sites. (34)

The library world is on its way to accommodating this mind-set with federated and broadcast search tools that comb multiple databases and catalogs from a single query. Even when searching within an individual proprietary database like Ebsco's MAS Ultra School Edition, a teen can find journal articles, images, primary sources, pamphlets, and reference sources.

At the present time, however, there is no genuinely *universal* search tool, no bona fide one-stop shopping. Technical limitations prevent web search engines from achieving total saturation of the free Web. They can neither continually crawl every web server that is online nor penetrate the free resources that are hidden behind database walls, such as library catalogs and archives. One good example of the latter is the Library of Congress's American Memory service (http://memory.loc.gov), which includes seven million primary-source documents scattered across more than a hundred collections. Finally, it goes without saying that Google and its cohorts cannot yet touch the contents of proprietary information resources. Teens (and probably most other searchers) have little awareness of this lack of universality in searching different types of sources.

As educators, we need to ensure that teens have a sense of the actual breadth and depth of the information landscape, the importance of that vastness, and the steps required to uncover what hides behind formal and informal information-retrieval systems. As they search for information, teens must be cognizant of the differences between the free Web and the deep Web. Additionally, they need to appreciate the enormity of the nondigitized information world. When it comes to selecting and evaluating information, we have an opportunity to capitalize on teens' format agnosticism, and to validate their instinctive belief that format is a superficial attribute. It is *not* terribly important if an article appears on a website or in a print journal. It *is* important to consider the nature of the article's authorship. Who wrote it? Why was it written? Who authorized and sponsored its publication? Questions like these keep teens' eyes on the prize, on the nature of authorship and intent, and therefore on the true value of the source.

FORMAL AND INFORMAL REVISITED

Here, at the frontier of format agnosticism, is where the conversation comes back to the issues discussed in the first two chapters of this book: the tensions between formal and informal information systems, the library and the Internet, the off-line and the online worlds. The distinctions among these worlds are becoming less clear (and less meaningful) every day. Perhaps the time is ripe for us to make the tensions both irrelevant and instructive by exploring ways we can use them to enlighten and inform.

When "Easy" Does Not Mean "Transparent"

As arcane as formal library search systems may seem, students need to be aware that the inner workings of commercial web search engines are also shrouded in mystery, but of a more suspect type. Search-engine relevance criteria are protected trade secrets. As noted in chapter 2, the search engine community has no membership-based cataloging and classification committees to propose and debate standards in a public forum, no Library of Congress to establish consistency and uniformity in descriptive practice and terminology. Instead, search engine algorithms constantly shift in response to technical developments and marketplace factors. Services like searchenginewatch.com are useful for keeping up-to-date with some of these changes, but staying current requires continual monitoring on the part of the user.

Still, users can generally count on certain commonly employed relevance-determination principles, such as the occurrence of key terms in metadata and text, the high incidence of links to a site, and more frequent crawling of sites that are updated often. But when significant changes occur in the web environment, they can wreak havoc with these established protocols. For example, once blogs began to proliferate, particularly as they started being syndicated, the frequency of self-referencing and cross-linking in them skewed the results of search-engine relevance criteria. Blogs began to dominate search-engine results lists. Google quietly developed strategies for identifying blogs and assigning them lower rankings.

The shady factor in search-engine results lists arises when rankings have less to do with relevance than they do with revenue generation for search engine companies and their clients. Website owners can pay to ensure that their site appears in search results, a technique called paid inclusion. Or, by purchasing paid placement rights, they can even guarantee that their site will appear high on a list of results. Advertisers can also "lease" keywords. Every time a user types in those words, the advertiser's links appear as sponsored links alongside the list of search results. I have asked my students to imagine publishers or authors inserting sponsored bibliographic records alongside catalog search results, or paid placement citations edging out other citations at the top of their database search results lists. This prospect highlights how accustomed we have all become to the commercial nature of the "free" Web.

Demystifying the Process

Sometimes I think I am the only librarian left in America who still teaches teens how to use the print version of the *Readers' Guide to Periodical Literature*. Why do I persist? Besides some purely pragmatic issues (e.g., the lack of sufficient numbers of computers for students to use to access the electronic version in my library), one reason is the portrayal of the venerable index in an old video called *How to Use the Readers' Guide* (1987). In one pivotal scene of this video, an indexer examines an article and assigns subject headings to it. After watching (and laughing at) this portrayal of ancient library times, the students in my classes enjoy identifying elements that have changed since its production, from hairstyles to computer hardware. But an essential ingredient remains the same—the use of human indexers who still personally index every article that is cited in each of the H. W. Wilson Company's print and electronic database products. Even the most naive among my students realize that automated search engine processing cannot come close to the quality and judgment of the human brain for this task.

The fact that I use this old video, or even the *Readers' Guide*, to teach this lesson is not so important. Other search tools and different teaching hooks would work just as well, as long as they illuminate a couple of important points. One of these points is that the inner workings of some long-standing library-world finding tools are quite transparent, in contrast to the secretive world of search engine protocols. Another point is that lessons like these can help students develop very useful mental models about indexes and databases. When we sort a stack of our library's periodicals into those which are indexed by *Readers' Guide* and those which are not, the students see physical evidence of its scope. When we separate out periodicals that are indexed by other database services, the students begin to have a sense of databases as a whole new and diverse world. And when we talk about the chances of finding the articles that are in these periodicals through a Google or AskJeeves search, they begin to understand the profound differences between the free Web and the deep Web. The point of this type of instruction is to lay bare the infrastructure and focus of search tools, enabling students to select and use them intelligently.

INTEGRATION

Just how we accomplish our instruction varies considerably, in part because the territory is so variable. One of the unanticipated consequences of today's rich information landscape is the necessity of working in so many different search environments. We are past the days when all we had to think about were the card catalog, a couple of periodical indexes, and our reference collection. Nowadays the tools are innumerable and overlapping, with most containing both formal and informal structural elements. Many are hybrid creations, featuring both bibliographic data and full-text and multimedia content. At least nonfederated information services (by far the majority) still come with labels or instructions that reflect their attributes. The *Readers' Guide to Periodical Literature* is, as it says, an index to periodical literature. But with most search tools (including *Readers' Guide*) now being served by the Web, they assume a superficial similarity to the point that users can lose track of what they are searching. This environment, an ironic mix of uniformity and complexity, creates special considerations for acquiring searching and content evaluation skills.

Searching

For all the reasons covered in chapter 2, searching effectively for information in any environment remains a skill that requires much analytical thought. The strategy used to search a bibliographic index like *Readers' Guide* produces different results when applied to its full-text online counterpart, and different results yet again when applied to the open-ended free Web. Students who are accustomed to searching the Web with standard search engines tend to carry over the same strategies when using other search tools. In practice, this means they clutter their searches with the extremely specific terminology that works so well in Google. A web search for "causes of earthquakes in California" yields a plethora of results, but falls flat when applied to a bibliographic database. For the latter, searchers need to move to a higher level of abstraction, removing adjectival terms like "causes" or "effects," and including only those nounlike terms the system is likely to recognize. And this strategy has not yet even taken the prospect of controlled vocabulary into consideration.

Teaching with concrete examples can help establish the mental models that searchers need as they move from one search environment to another. I sometimes ask students to open a book at random and read a sentence from it. Could they find the book in the library's catalog by looking under the words in that sentence? No. They immediately recognize the futility of that particular strategy. Instead, they have to think in terms of what the *whole* book is about, abstract its subject to two or three key terms or phrases, and then look in the catalog under those terms. What about the web environment? Could they find their book by searching Google for the words in that sentence? Unlikely. Realization begins to dawn that the book's entire contents are probably not digitized and are therefore not searchable. By extrapolation, neither are the vast majority of the books in the library (or the bookstore, or on the shelves at home). Even as Google and other Internet search providers collaborate with research libraries and publishers to digitize books, it will be a long time before current, copyrighted books are routinely searchable and freely available online (Markoff and Wyatt 2004).

Computer and information scientists, as well as web content providers, are working feverishly to make natural language and full-text searching more feasible. Amazon has its "Search Inside" feature, in which customers can search the full text of a rapidly growing number of book titles. Amazon's subsidiary, A9.com, allows simultaneous searches of the Web and Amazon's book database. A search on "Alicia Svigals," one of today's foremost klezmer music violinists, displays her personal website right at the top of A9's web results list, and the sites that immediately follow are all relevant. Her search results from the book database seem almost magical. Because Svigals has not (yet) been the subject of a biography or written a book herself, all the hits that appear indicate places where she is a subject *within the contents* of other books. These books are, for the most part, general titles about modern klezmer or world music. Each entry includes an excerpt that mentions her, citing the page number on which it appears. (See figure 8-1.)

One of the titles on this results list is a book called *Jewish Mothers: Strength, Wisdom, and Compassion*, which profiles fifty American Jewish women, from the first woman rabbi hired by a major Conservative congregation to the puppeteer

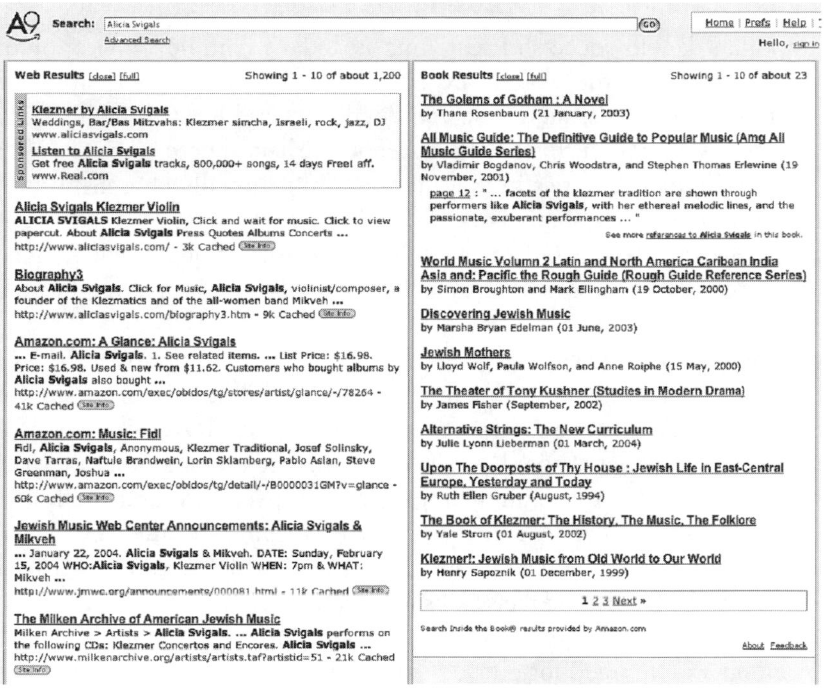

FIGURE 8-1

Results of an A9 search on klezmer violinist Alicia Svigals, showing Web
results on the left side of the page and book results on the right side.

Shari Lewis. That Alicia Svigals is one of these women is no surprise, but a
searcher could only discover this by using a search tool such as A9.com. A library
catalog would not suffice, since the five very general Library of Congress subject
headings assigned to the book are along the lines of "Mothers -- United States --
Interviews" and "Jewish Women -- United States -- Social conditions -- 20th
century."

On the other hand, the lack of vocabulary control in these full-text searches
can produce extremely imprecise results. The search in A9.com on "causes of
earthquakes in California" retrieves some relevant hits, but near the top of the list
appear titles like *The Portable MBA* and *Light His Fire: How to Keep Your Man
Passionately and Hopelessly in Love with You*. Finally, if this book is ever included
in Amazon's "Search Inside" database, those looking for information on Alicia
Svigals will wonder why they retrieved a book on teenagers and technology.

Focusing the Scope

An important key to successful searching in today's complex environment is to focus the scope of the search by subdividing it into manageable chunks. Specialized search tools, such as search directories and website "collections," are a chief means by which this has been accomplished. These website collections resemble traditional libraries in that items are intentionally chosen in much the same way as books in a library are chosen. The sites that are selected fit within a defined collection scope and meet certain standards of quality. Searchers need not be concerned about hidden factors like paid placement that might influence qualitative rankings.

Some directory services are nonprofit efforts, like the Librarian's Index to the Internet (http://lii.org), which contains approximately 14,000 websites in its database, and the Internet Scout Report (http://scout.wisc.edu/Reports/ScoutReport/Current/), a little larger at about 17,000 websites. Their annotations are written by outside reviewers, librarians, and subject matter specialists, and neither service accepts advertising. Other directory services are creations of the web community itself, such as the Open Directory (http://dmoz.org), which is edited by volunteers. The search industry also markets website directories, such as Thinkronize's K–12 NetTrekker product (http://www.nettrekker.com/). Subscription fees, in these cases, eliminate the need for outside advertising. Even with 180,000 websites in the NetTrekker database, its search universe is considerably smaller than the free Web and its content is ostensibly value-added by being targeted to the school audience and vetted by teacher-selectors.

There is an important side note to add here about searching, a problem briefly referred to in chapter 2. Although web directories connect searchers to web content, users are actually searching bibliographic databases rather than full-content websites. But web directories *look* like search engines, with their search window prominently displayed, and users often expect them to *act* like search engines. (See figure 8-2.) Users will experience the same type of level-of-specificity problems described earlier if their searches are constructed too narrowly. Searching on "causes of earthquakes in California" in the Librarian's Index to the Internet yields one hit, the California Governor's Office of Emergency Services, which does not really describe the causes of earthquakes. But a search on "earthquakes California" yields thirty-four hits, many of which contain information about the causes of earthquakes there.

Searchers can also use databases of various types to focus the search universe. In addition to ensuring some level of quality, databases use other focusing criteria such as subject (e.g., subject-specialized databases), audience (e.g., scholars, the K–12 market, the business community, etc.), and publication type (e.g., journal

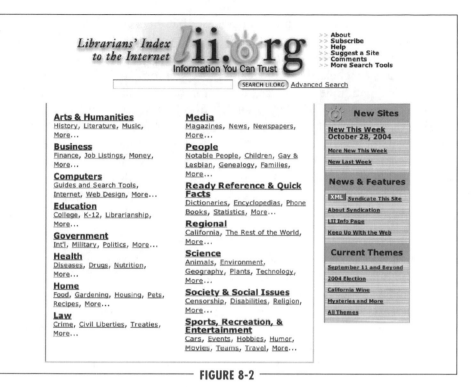

FIGURE 8-2

Home page of the Librarians' Index to the Internet, featuring the search box at the top followed by subject categories below.

articles rather than websites). Quality control is not guaranteed. Students may not realize that there are significant qualitative differences between a free database site like findarticles.com and a subscription database like OCLC FirstSearch's Wilson Select Plus. Both purport to index a wide variety of periodical resources. But the findarticles.com database is filled with trade journals and public relations releases and its indexing schedule lags significantly. Wilson Select Plus is updated weekly and includes important periodical titles ranging from *Time* magazine to the *Journal of Atmospheric and Oceanic Technology*.

Some databases are hybrid types, their content encompassing bibliographic periodical records as well as full-text websites. For example, Elsevier's science database Scirus (http://www.scirus.com) consists of websites as well as journal articles, and it also includes non-Elsevier content, such as portions of the National Library of Medicine's PubMed database. Access to Scirus is free, though access to the full text of the articles from its Science Direct component is fee-based, which makes Scirus an interesting case of a database that indexes both the free web and the invisible Web. The company's likely business model is that profits from the full-text service subsidize free access to the bibliographic information.

Librarians also help their clientele focus the information universe by providing them with pathfinders, research guides, and other traditional tools of the trade. Today, library websites have an especially important role in supporting the user's search experience. Well-designed sites can be customized to meet the needs, interests, and cultural backgrounds of the community. Library websites eliminate the clutter of commercial web portals and contain links to value-added services that only a library can offer, such as their proprietary databases. Given this potential, Walter Minkel, former technology editor of *School Library Journal*, wonders at so many school librarians' habits of placing prominent links to Google on their websites:

> Yeah, it's easy to get a Google logo and search box from www.google.com to put on your site. But think about the message you're sending. When students arrive at your home page, instead of being directed first to your catalog, databases, or a list of recommended Web sites that are ideal for their assignments, they immediately see a link to Google. You're saying, in effect, "Sorry, the library can't really help you. Instead of visiting our site, why don't you visit Google and poke through its 3,083,324,652 Web pages on your own?" (Minkel 2003, 37)

At the Public Library of Charlotte and Mecklenburg County (N.C.), users can actually create a personalized version of the library's website to suit their own needs. This service, called brarydog (http://www.brarydog.net), allows users to add their favorite links to an already structured set of free and subscription-based resources, and to even alter the look of the page by selecting background image and color. The page is available to them wherever they have Internet access.

Students can learn techniques that will help them focus the search process for themselves. Many already use web browser bookmarks as signposts or trail markers to chart their way through a cluttered Internet landscape (Harris Interactive 2003). Marylaine Block (2001, 34) suggests prompting students to use "wedge words," words that tell search engines what *categories* of sites are wanted. For example, if topic X is combined with "FAQ" (or "encyclopedia," "expert," "law," "forum," and so on), chances are good that the search results will predominantly consist of FAQ sites.

Another useful strategy, mentioned briefly at the close of the previous chapter, is to require students to develop their own pathfinders, either as precursors to research projects, as ends in themselves, or as guides for others. Though the pathfinder process is a focusing exercise, it also pushes students into using a wider variety of sources than they otherwise might. Librarian Joyce Valenza's template for student-created pathfinders prompts students to consider including associations, experts, blogs, image resources, and primary source materials, as well as standard elements like subject headings, print and online indexes, Internet subject directories, specific websites, and call number ranges (2003b, 109–10; online template available at http://mciu.org/~spjvweb/pathfinder.html). Students must begin with an introduction to the topic and a statement describing the scope of the pathfinder's coverage, exercises which encourage meta-cognition and reflection about the task.

Selection and Evaluation

Just as young searchers tend to employ singular *search* strategies across different types of search environments, they also fall back on familiar *selection* habits. In her study of fifth-graders' use of an online catalog, an electronic encyclopedia, an electronic magazine index, and the Web, Hirsh (1999) found that students rely heavily on the title (of the book, the article, or the website) to determine usefulness. They scan the descriptive information and skim lead paragraphs and tables of contents. They give great weight to information that matches their own search terms or the teacher's terminology, no matter what the source. Like many teens, they are uncritical of the information they find, trusting its veracity regardless of media type. If the information is on topic, it is "good."

The scanning and skimming behaviors exhibited by these fifth-graders demonstrate a good starting strategy, but are obviously not sufficient to the task. Term matching does not necessarily signify the worthiness of a source, and sometimes not even its topicality. Older students, having developed beyond the concrete thinking stage, ought to be able to apply multiple selection criteria and triangulate the evidence they find. And they do, spending much of their time "separating the wheat from the chaff" (Harris Interactive 2003, 17). But the challenges facing them are considerable. In today's information environment, students must first understand the structure of an information source before its content can be meaningfully evaluated. And this task can be fraught with complication. The following is an example that illustrates the roadblocks students must navigate.

"I FOUND IT ON THE INTERNET"

When one of my students conducted a web search on women in the military, she found an article titled "Women at Arms" (http://www.policyreview.org/aug00/Bockhorn.html). (See figure 8-3.) As far as she was concerned, this page was a source she found on the Internet, undifferentiated from other web-based sources.

She did not recognize it as a piece from the online counterpart of a scholarly print journal, *Policy Review.* To some degree, the website's designers are responsible for her misconception. Though the *Policy Review* masthead is unmistakable, the links on the page lead to the journal's current issue, not to the August 2000 issue in which the article originally appeared. The original issue can only be accessed by deleting Bockhorn.html from the URL, not a very intuitive navigational method. My student cited this source as a web page, not as an article in a journal. While she documented some of the important information—the title of the piece, the author's name, and the URL that would lead other readers to her source—she missed important contextual information that would have helped her interpret its value.

FIGURE 8-3

Book review on the website of *Policy Review,* a journal published by the Hoover Institution at Stanford University.

The next problem in deciphering this source is that it is not, after all, really an article about women in the military. Instead, it is an extended editorial review of two books on the topic. A bibliography generation tool like NoodleBib, with its detailed prompts, or timely input from a teacher or librarian, might have pushed my student to make this discovery. And, still, she would not have been finished with her detective work. From the online table-of-contents page of the issue, there is a link to the publisher of *Policy Review,* the Hoover Institution at Stanford University (in a short-lived collaboration with the Heritage Foundation, a conservative think tank). A little digging uncovers the Hoover Institution's mission, one which is likely to shape (i.e., bias) the content of its publications. To be thorough, my student would have had to parse out the meaning of that mission and the degree to which it affected her planned use of the source. She would also have needed to weigh the usefulness of a book review for her needs. In the end, she could regard the article as a "bread crumb" source, one she could not use outright but which would lead her to other sources she could use, such as the books being reviewed. To get that far, she would have had to read an article she would not get "credit" for and then search again, this time for the two books.

Not many students would persist through all the steps just described. Efforts like these are generally not rewarded by teachers and are often not even acknowledged. They are discounted as merely an inevitable occurrence in the indefinable task that is library research. But if students are expected to demonstrate good judgment in selecting sources, the search process must be given its due. This can be accomplished by constructing rubrics that credit detection and analysis work, assigning students to maintain research journals to promote reflective thinking, and otherwise making the process as important as the product. The goal is to develop thoughtful habits of mind that serve the user throughout adulthood.

FORGING NEW PATHWAYS

So far in this chapter, I have focused on the information world, emphasizing its marvelous richness and its confounding complexity. But information technology is only half of the ICT puzzle and, as discussed in earlier chapters, *communication* technology is the key to the modern teenager's heart. For teens, "communication technology" is not a noun but a verb; it is the fundamental way these "technology natives" interact (NetDay 2004, 21). Yet teens encounter many obstacles to the use of communication technologies at school and in public institutions, places in which they spend a considerable proportion of their lives. It is time to assemble a more integrated ICT library environment for them. Doing so means imagining libraries in a new light and facing change in proactive ways.

Changing Roles for Libraries and Librarians

The ICT-powered library can simply be thought of as one which uses new technology tools to provide core services in a rapidly changing world. An effective ICT presence in libraries can ensure that teens, because they are comfortable in today's libraries, will become tomorrow's library users and supporters. But the impact of changing ICTs on the roles of librarians and libraries cannot be discounted either. Library technology writer Marylaine Block, who edited a book called *Net Effects: How Librarians Can Manage the Unintended Consequences of the Internet* (2003), prescribes remedies for librarians who feel they are losing ground. She discusses regaining control over selection by creating web indexes, databases, and search engines. She tells us that the book can be rescued through user-friendly cataloging, reading and outreach programs, and new promotional models such as library blogs. She allots an entire chapter to training users and another chapter to training ourselves.

Block also devotes considerable space to Jenny Levine's "shifted librarian" model, which has come to signify meeting users on their own terms and with their tools of choice. The clientele of today and tomorrow, the Net Generation (or NetGens), has a profoundly different approach to information, as Levine herself articulates:

> To my mind, *the biggest difference is that they expect information to come to them, whether it's via the Web, email, cell phone, online chat, whatever.* And given the tip of the iceberg of technology we're seeing, *it's going to have a big impact on how they expect to receive library services,* which means librarians have to start adjusting now. I call that adjustment "shifting" because I think you have to start meeting these kids' information needs *in their world,* not yours. *The library has to become more portable or "shifted"* [author's emphases]. (http://www.theshifted librarian.comstories/2002/01/19/whatIsAShiftedLibrarian.html)

In Levine's vision, books and other traditional services still occupy center stage, but they are given a boost from new modes of communication and service delivery. This expanded repertoire comes in many guises, such as value-added websites, blogs that support user interests and needs, chat reference services, and other personalized electronic services like the brarydog service of the Public Library of Charlotte and Mecklenburg County.

GIVE 'EM WHAT THEY WANT

Does the "shifted librarian" model mean turning the library into a mall or an arcade? The concern about sacrificing quality to meet popular demand is an old one, hearkening back to the development of early public libraries as places for self-improvement rather than as places to exchange dime novels. In the more recent

1980s, Charles Robinson and the staff of the Baltimore County Public Library (BCPL) raised the hackles of the library profession when they launched the notorious "Give 'em what they want!" campaign (Rawlinson 1981). The gist of the model was that public money should be spent on what the public wanted, not on what librarians thought the public ought to have. The epicenter of the controversy was collection development, with the BCPL committing a substantial proportion of its dollars to purchasing the types of materials that would generate high circulation. Critics decried what they saw as a "McLibrary" approach, in which centralized selection and catering to the (perceived) lowest common denominator threatened to eradicate the personalized services, specialized skills, and pedagogical role that had been the pride of the profession.

Judging by this debate, it is an easy stretch to imagine a worst-case "shifted library" scenario, in which a library offers only the ICT services the public appears to want. Its young adult space would be populated with zombie-like teens sitting at computers, instant messaging without apparent purpose, blasting music, playing raucous video games, and downloading pornographic images. Nary a book nor a librarian in sight. However, "shifted" does not have to mean the abandonment, or even a compromise, of principles. It is important to remember that technology itself is value-neutral. Even its use can be neutral, depending upon the situational and contextual factors that surround it. But if technology is neither inherently good nor bad, it does require careful management. The shifted library can therefore be a hard sell at administrative levels, but the potential for reward is great.

One example of a successful large-scale implementation is the Seattle Public Library's Central Library branch (http://www.spl.org), where the crayon-colored, futuristic architectural design personifies the library's retooled services. Users do not have to run from one reference desk to another in pursuit of information. Instead, the library has a central Mixing Chamber, a "trading floor for information," staffed by subject specialists. These librarians have access to the usual print and electronic reference tools, and are also equipped with wireless communication devices that allow them to be in touch with other specialists as needed. Dumbwaiters, a reliable form of old technology, deliver materials to them from the "Book Spiral." The library's Starbucks Teen Center, in addition to offering traditional bread-and-butter services like collections targeted to teen interests, features "sound domes for a music experience," group project rooms, Internet access and software, and classes and workshops designed specifically for teens.

For most practitioners (i.e., those of us who do not work at Seattle's Central Library), what does it actually mean to become "shifted"? First, librarians need to become knowledgeable about ICTs, to know which ones are being used by area teens, and how they are being used. Next, dabble a bit and test the waters. Having personal experience with a new ICT makes it much easier to understand those who are avid users of it. I began to use instant messaging as an additional way to stay in touch with my husband and my grown kids. But my "coolness" stock at school rose considerably when I made my screen name public. I was surprised by the number of students who messaged me to say hi, to chat, and, yes, to even ask library-related questions. Any initial awkwardness I felt with the technology was soon eclipsed by the benefits it brought me.

The next step is to allow teens their tools in libraries in ways that are feasible and useful to them. First, libraries need to provide room for both multitasking and non-multitasking behaviors, establishing parameters that make sense for all users of the library, including staff. Librarians working with teens are in a position to educate their colleagues about why multitasking behaviors in the library should be supported and what policies can be implemented to make them work (Braun 2004). Huge changes are not required. Merely allowing a teen to plug headphones into a sound-capable computer is one inexpensive, low-impact example. Those who wish to listen to music while working can do so; those who would rather not, can skip it.

Multitasking aside, some ICT tools, such as instant messaging and gaming, initially appear to be unsuitable for any library setting. But some of our exemplary shifted librarians have learned otherwise. For example, Rebecca Purdy (2002, 104) argues that instant messaging and chat protocols have a place in the public library setting: "Chatting is not against the law, and it shouldn't be against library rules. Limit the amount of time on the computer, not appropriate personal use." She suggests that librarians assume a proactive role by providing safety tips on their websites, sponsoring programs on ICT uses and abuses, and developing handouts on chat room safety.

Michele Gorman (2002) describes how the Wired for Youth centers at the Austin (Tex.) Public Library integrate nontraditional computing activities into an environment that still assigns priority to homework and other core library activities. She notes that computer games have become a gateway activity for kids who are typically non-library users, which is a huge payoff. Playing games on the Internet helps these teens feel comfortable with the computer and within the library environment. They gradually sign up for other activities like computer classes, and begin to use other software for schoolwork and for fun. Gorman's experience is not an isolated one. The February 2005 issue of *Voice of Youth Advocates* was devoted to the topic of gaming in the library setting.

IT'S NOT ALL CANDY: ADAPTING TRADITIONAL SERVICES

Despite what critics had to say about the "Give 'em what they want!" campaign at the Baltimore County Public Library, the classics always maintained a strong presence on the shelves there. The same thing can be said for service "classics" in the shifted library. In fact, ICTs have always been used to enhance core library services, from the first online union catalogs to today's e-mail delivery of interlibrary loan articles. Of course, the road to change is not always a smooth one. Virtual (i.e., chat) reference service is an interesting example of a somewhat rocky adaptation of a traditional service. In this case, one service is actually catching up with another—remote users are now getting help with the remote resources that have already been made available to them. The pacing and lingo of virtual interactions can be challenging for those who are not accustomed to communicating online, in real time. The librarians who were early adopters of the service felt compelled to answer immediately, as they did for in-person or telephone reference transactions.

Kelly Broughton (2001) describes how she adjusted to the new milieu by observing her teenage child chat online, noting that IM conversations are often punctuated with long silences. She realized that instant messagers are accustomed to delays as an artifact of multitasking. It became clear to her that when her virtual clientele were asking reference questions online, they were also likely to be engaged in several other activities at the same time. Broughton soon learned to relax about being interrupted during virtual reference sessions and to "speak" in short bursts rather than long paragraphs.

Adaptations to core teaching activities are also inevitable in ICT-enhanced environments. Assessment techniques, for example, need to be modified. It takes a different skill set to grade websites than it does to grade term papers. Class discussions must be handled differently in the online environment than they are in the classroom. During in-class discussions, students can see one another's facial expressions and the teacher can control the flow of conversation by calling on individuals. Online class discussion may have to be more structured to produce desired learning outcomes (Murray 2000). Students need to learn to quote one another appropriately to provide their peers with sufficient context for new comments. Without being directed to summarize one another's responses and provide specific feedback, students tend to simply exchange speeches. In other words, "listening" online requires just as much effort, if not more, as does listening in face-to-face interactions. Again, the potential payoff of the new environment is high. Students who do not ordinarily speak out in class may do so online. Online discussions have fewer time restrictions; no bells are going to ring.

Some new ICTs seem tailor-made for libraries. Blogs have great potential for enhancing traditional services. Technology maven Pam Berger (2003, 2) expresses this opinion about their usefulness in the school library environment:

> In school libraries, blogs are an extension of what we already do: identify, organize, and make information accessible. Blogs let us do it in a timely fashion. It

gives us an opportunity to be more responsive, to reach out to the faculty and students via our library blogs to highlight news, post student/faculty book reviews and invite comments, announce events, list new acquisitions, etc.

Why blogs as opposed to other types of interactive web services? Blog software providers have made blogs easy to set up and maintain, inexpensive to run (if not actually free), and inviting for target audiences. Their format is recognizable to teens, who immediately know how to follow the banter and participate in the discussions.

Successful education-related blog implementations are on the rise, as evidenced by collaborative support sites like the Educational Bloggers Network (http://www.ebn.weblogger.com). Blogs present all sorts of opportunities for school librarians to collaborate with teachers. Embrey (2002) describes a hypothetical ecology project in which students explain their hypothesis in an initial blog post and then use subsequent postings to report their routine observations of changes in a local river. The blog is their central clearinghouse for posting links to other sites that reference the river's history and impact. The students also use a news aggregator (similar to a personalized news wire service) to track news items that are relevant to their project and then post links to those on the blog. Finally, they syndicate their own blog, so that news aggregators distribute the results of their efforts to other interested parties.

Other examples of service enhancements are plentiful, many of which were described in chapter 3. Teachers use e-mail and websites to communicate with parents, post assignments, and provide links to important course-related information. More teachers are using web-supported coursework software, which students use to complete assignments, take tests, and participate in discussions. Librarians and teachers collaborate in developing ICT-based assignments and resources. On their own, students use all manner of homework help sites, from "Ask an Expert" services to (the sometimes infamous) literature summary and analysis sites like Sparknotes.com. As previously noted, student products have evolved as well. Instead of traditional term papers and reports, students are often asked to use a blend of technology-based multimedia and communication tools to synthesize and present information.

ETHICS "R" NOW-MORE-THAN-EVER US

Librarians are still *the* information specialists. But if librarians are *only* information specialists, particularly if they work with teens, they are not fulfilling their charge. It is also the librarian's job to teach the responsible use of information, which these days encompasses both information and communication technologies. Although librarians have a long history of teaching ethics, its scope has typically been limited to the traditional confines of plagiarism and copyright lessons. The American Association of School Librarians and the Association of Educational Communications and Technology codified librarians' ethics education responsibility in the 1998 *Information Literacy Standards for Student Learning*. Standard 8 describes the information-literate student as one who "practices ethical behavior in regard to information and information technology" (American Association of School Librarians 1998, 36). The new standards expand the scope of our traditional territory and make ethics education a core responsibility of librarians.

There are compelling reasons why librarians should take a lead role in teaching ICT ethics. In both school and public libraries, librarians are in a position to see the whole ICT picture and the relationship teens have to it. Content, behavior, and management issues are all part of the librarian's purview. It would therefore be counterproductive *not* to assist teens in understanding the complications and consequences of the ICT environment. In the public library setting, who else will take care of this if not the librarian? At school, other stakeholders have their own interests to pursue. The science teacher is likely to teach science ICT applications and resources, the French teacher is likely to teach French ICT applications and resources, and so on. Even the computer teacher is likely to focus on technical skills and, if technology ethics are taught at all, may neglect the information ethics component. Only the school librarian's priorities are, by definition, focused on the big picture.

In chapter 7 I described how schools and libraries employ three basic strategies in managing ICT disciplinary issues: regulatory, technological, and pedagogical. For the most part, and possibly in self-defense, we seem to regard the first two as being well within our domain. No one questions whether or not librarians should be involved in setting policies for acceptable Internet use or making decisions about security and filtering software. But the pedagogical role is one that librarians have seemed hesitant to assume. I find this reluctance puzzling. Perhaps it exists because librarians have a professional Library Bill of Rights (that of the American Library Association) which instills a kind of hands-off attitude; respecting users' rights to privacy and promoting open access to information are sacred trusts. But upholding those principles does not mean that librarians do not also have a responsibility to introduce ethics concepts to their users. In fact, in today's complex world, information skills are so closely associated with moral principles that one is hard to teach without the other. Librarians have a new sacred trust, which is to teach teens to become responsible as well as intelligent citizens in the virtual and physical worlds.

SUGGESTIONS FOR EFFECTIVE LIBRARIANS

Librarians have always been involved in literacy efforts, and ICT literacy is no exception. In her overview of recent literacy movements, June Pullen Weis (2004) comments on the growing mainstreaming of ICT literacy. Unlike previous literacy initiatives, including librarians' own information-literacy bandwagon, "ICT literacy is recognized by a wide range of global stakeholders, including K–12 education, postsecondary education, and business and government leaders" (14). She feels the time is right for the key players to collaboratively articulate common definitions and implement shared goals. This is good news for librarians, who have an important opportunity to influence the development of ICT education. But first, librarians must understand the changes wrought by ICTs and, as today's teens would say, *own* them. In other words, we need to take what is handed to us and shape it into a force that promotes the core values of librarianship.

Those core values continue to be important. Principals, legislators, students, teachers, and anyone who has an opinion on the subject have been known to pose the question: "Why do we need a librarian or a library when we have the Internet?" Kahn and Mallette (2002) asked the librarians on an electronic discussion list how they would answer this question and collected some snappy comebacks. "If we have dictionaries, why do we need English teachers?" "Why do people read *TV Guide*? They can change channels all they want." And my favorite: "Why would we want to spend ten minutes looking something up in a book when we can spend two hours looking for it on the Web?" The authors, of course, follow up these barbs with longer, quite thoughtful answers to the question. In short, librarians are still needed because "everything" is not on the Internet and because librarians are trained to find the most appropriate information, regardless of format.

Librarians do much more than just help people find information. We teach, we bring the magic of discovery to small (and large) children, we help people connect to one another, we provide a sense of place in our facilities. Today, librarians have the power to make the merger of information and communication technologies work *for* people in ways that are humane and enriching. Teenagers are our partners in this endeavor. They are the innovators whose imaginations we must value. We will not succeed without their vision and energy, and they will not become library users without our skill and passion. It's a marriage made in heaven.

REFERENCES

Abram, Stephen, and Judy Luther. 2004. Born with the chip. *Library Journal* 129 (8): 34–37.

Agosto, Denise E. 2002. Bounded rationality and satisficing in young people's web-based decision making. *Journal of the American Society for Information Science* 53 (1): 16–27.

Aho, James A. 1990. *The politics of righteousness: Idaho Christian patriotism.* Seattle: University of Washington Press.

Allen, Katherine, and Lee Rainie. 2002. Parents online. Pew Internet and American Life Project. http://www.pewinternet.org/ PPF/r/75/report_display.asp.

American Association of School Librarians and Association of Educational Communications and technology. 1998. *Information literacy standards for student learning.* Chicago: American Library Association.

American Library Association. Library Bill of Rights. http://www.ala.org/ala/oif/statementspols/statementsif/librarybillrights.htm.

Anti-Defamation League. Responding to extremist speech online: 10 frequently asked questions. http://www.adl.org/issue_combating_hate/10faq_extremist_online.asp.

Association for Library Collections and Technical Services. 2003. Final report of the Subcommittee on Subject Reference Structures in Automated Systems. http://www.ala.org/Content/ContentGroups/ALCTS1/Cataloging_and_Classification_Section/Committees3/Subject_Analysis/Subject_Reference_Structures/Subject_Reference_Structures.htm.

———. n.d. SAC Task Force on Library of Congress Subject Heading Revisions Relating to the Poor People's Policy. Report on proposed headings. http://

www.ala.org/Content/ContentGroups/ALCTS1/Cataloging_and
_Classification_Section/Committees3/Subject_Analysis/LC_TF/ppp.pdf.

Berger, Pam. 2003. Are you blogging yet? *Information Searcher* 14 (2): 1–4.

Berman, Sanford. 1984. C'mon guys, lighten up! *Technicalities* 4 (12): 9. Also published in Berman, Sanford. 1988. *Worth noting: Editorials, letters, essays, and interview, and bibliography*. Jefferson, NC: McFarland.

———. 1987. The terrible truth about teenlit cataloging. *Top of the News* 43 (3): 311–320. Also published in Berman, Sanford. 1988. *Worth noting: Editorials, letters, essays, and interview, and bibliography*. Jefferson, NC: McFarland.

———. 1993. *Prejudices and antipathies: A tract on the LC subject heads concerning people*. Jefferson, NC: McFarland.

Block, Marylaine. 2001. Teaching kids indirectly. *Library Journal NetConnect*, Summer, 33–34.

———, ed. 2003. *Net effects: How librarians can manage the unintended consequences of the Internet*. Medford, NJ: Information Today.

Blood, Rebecca. 2002. *The Weblog handbook: Practical advice on creating and maintaining your blog*. Cambridge, MA: Perseus.

Borgman, Christine L., et al. 1995. Children's searching behavior on browsing and keyword online catalogs: The Science Library Catalog Project. *Journal of the American Society for Information Science* 46 (9): 663–84.

Branch, Jennifer. 2002. Helping students become better electronic searchers. *Teacher Librarian* 30 (1): 14–18.

Braun, Linda W. 2004. Multitasking in the library. *Voice of Youth Advocates* 27 (2): 111.

Broughton, Kelly. 2001. Our experiment in online real-time reference. *Computers in Libraries* 21 (4): 26–31.

Bruce, Bertram C. 2003. Open source: Everyone becomes a printer. In *Literacy in the information age: Inquiries into meaning making with new technologies*, ed. Bertram C. Bruce. Newark, DE: International Reading Association, 100–106.

Bruce, Harry. 2002. *The user's view of the Internet*. Lanham, MD: Scarecrow.

Budd, John. 1996. The complexity of information retrieval: A hypothetical example. *Journal of Academic Librarianship* 22 (March): 111–17.

Busey, Paula, and Tom Doerr. 1993. Kid's Catalog: An information retrieval system for children. *Journal of Youth Services in Libraries* 7 (1): 77–84.

Callahan, David. 2004. *The cheating culture: Why more Americans are doing wrong to get ahead*. Orlando, FL: Harcourt.

Case, Donald O. 2002. *Looking for information: A survey of research on information seeking, needs, and behavior*. San Diego: Academic Press.

Chelton, Mary K. 1999. Behavior of librarians in school and public libraries with adolescents: Implications for practice and LIS education. *Journal of Education in Library and Information Science* 40 (2): 99–111.

———. 2001. Young adults as problems: How the social construction of a marginalized user category occurs. *Journal of Education in Library and Information Science* 42 (1): 4–11.

———. 2002. The "problem patron" public libraries created. *The Reference Librarian* (75/76): 23–32.

The Christian Century. 2003. Teens break no-sex vows, study suggests: Some say oral sex not sex, 27 December, 14.

Cochrane, Pauline A. 1986. *Improving LCSH for use in online catalogs*. Littleton, CO: Libraries Unlimited.

Cutter, Charles A. 1876. Library catalogues. In *Public libraries in the United States of America: Their history, condition, and management*. Special report, Department of the Interior, Bureau of Education. Part 1. Washington, DC: U.S. Government Printing Office, 526–622.

Dervin, Brenda. 1976. Strategies for dealing with human information needs: Information or communication? *Journal of Broadcasting* 20 (3): 324–33.

Dewey, John. 1902. *The child and the curriculum*. Chicago: University of Chicago Press.

———. 1915. *The school and society*. Chicago: University of Chicago Press.

Dewey, Melvil. 1876. Catalogues and cataloguing, Part 1. In *Public libraries in the United States of America: Their history, condition, and management*. Special report, Department of the Interior, Bureau of Education. Part 1. Washington, DC: U.S. Government Printing Office, 623–48.

Dickerson, Chad. 2004. When games are more than child's play. *Infoworld*, 16 January. http://www.infoworld.com/article/04/01/16/03OPconnection_1 .html.

Drabenstott, Karen M., Schelle Simcox, and Eileen G. Fenton. 1999. End-user understanding of subject headings in library catalogs. *Library Resources and Technical Services* 43 (3): 140–60.

Dresang, Eliza T. 1999. More research needed: Informal information-seeking behavior of youth on the Internet. *Journal of the American Society for Information Science* 50 (12): 1123–24.

Durkheim, Émile. 1925/1961. *Moral education.* New York: Free Press.

Embrey, Theresa Ross. 2002. You blog, we blog: A guide to how teacher-librarians can use weblogs to build communication and research skills. *Teacher Librarian* 30 (2): 7–9.

Fidel, Raya, et al. 1999. A visit to the information mall: Web searching behavior of high school students. *Journal of the American Society for Information Science* 50 (1): 24–37.

Fisher, Danyel. 2003. Studying social information spaces. In *From Usenet to CoWebs: Interacting with social information spaces*, ed. Christopher Lueg and Danyel Fisher. London: Springer-Verlag, 3–19.

Foroohar, Rana. 2003. Don't be lame. *Newsweek*, 8 September, 10–11.

Fourie, Ina. 2002. How can we take a socio-cognitive approach in teaching indexing and abstracting? *The Indexer* 23 (2): 83–85.

Gibaldi, Joseph. 2003. *MLA handbook for writers of research papers.* 6th ed. New York: Modern Language Association.

Girl Scout Research Institute. 2002. *The net effect: Girls and the new media. Executive summary.* New York: Girl Scouts of the USA.

Gorman, Michele. 2002. Wiring teens to the library. *Library Journal NetConnect*, Summer, 18–20.

Grinter, Rebecca E., and Leysia Palen. 2002. Instant messaging in teen life. In *Proceedings of the ACM Conference on Computer Supported Cooperative Work*, New Orleans, LA.

Gross, Melissa. 1999. Imposed queries in the school library media center: A descriptive study. *Library and Information Science Research* 21 (4): 501–21.

Hagerty, Barbara Bradley. 2004. Teen-age Wiccans. *All Things Considered.* National Public Radio, 13 May.

Hamelink, Cees J. 2000. *The ethics of cyberspace.* London: Sage.

Harris Interactive and Teenage Research Unlimited. 2003. Born to be wired: The role of new media for a digital generation. Study commissioned by Yahoo! and Carat Interactive. http://promotions.yahoo.com/btbw_2003.

Hirsh, Sandra G. 1999. Children's relevance criteria and information seeking on electronic resources. *Journal of the American Society for Information Science* 50 (14): 1265–83.

How to use the Readers' Guide. 1987. Directed by Richard S. Blofson. 18 min. Produced by Visual Education for the H. W. Wilson Company. Videocassette.

Intelligence Report. 2004. Active hate websites in the United States in the year 2003. 113 (Spring): 43–49.

Johnson, Doug. 2003. *Learning right from wrong in the digital age: An ethics guide for parents, teachers, librarians, and others who care about computer-using young people.* Worthington, OH: Linworth.

Joinson, Adam N. 2003. *Understanding the psychology of Internet behaviour: Virtual worlds, real lives.* Basingstoke, UK: Palgrave Macmillan.

Jones, Steve. 2002. The Internet goes to college: How students are living in the future with today's technology. Pew Internet and American Life Project. http://www.pewinternet.org/PPF/r/71/report_display.asp.

Kahn, Cynthia, and Michelle Mallette. 2002. Why do we need a teacher-librarian or a library when we have the Internet? *Teacher Librarian* 29 (4): bonus online article. http://www.teacherlibrarian.com/tlmag/v_29/v_29_4 _feature_bonus.html.

Kanoff, Marjorie. 2003. *Youth illicit drug use prevention: DARE long-term evaluations and federal efforts to identify effective programs.* Washington, DC: General Accounting Office. Also available at http://www.gao.gov/new.items/ d03172r.pdf.

Kohlberg, Lawrence. 1958. The development of modes of moral thinking and choice in the years ten to sixteen. PhD diss., University of Chicago.

———. 1984. *The psychology of moral development: The nature and validity of moral stages.* Vol. 2, *Essays on moral development.* San Francisco: Harper and Row.

Krim, Jonathan. 2003. Pornography prevalent on file sharing services. *Washington Post,* 13 March, E01.

Kuhlthau, Carol C. 1997. Learning in digital libraries: An information search process. *Library Trends* 45 (4): 708–24.

———. 2004. *Seeking meaning: A process approach to library and information services.* 2nd ed. Westport, CT: Libraries Unlimited.

Landau, Elaine. 1986. *Different drummer: Homosexuality in America.* New York: Messner.

Lenhart, Amanda L., Lee Rainie, and Oliver Lewis. 2001. Teenage life online: The rise of the instant-message generation and the Internet's impact on friendships and family relationships. Pew Internet and American Life Project. http://207.21.232.103/PPF/r/36/report_display.asp.

Lenhart, Amanda, Maya Simon, and Mike Graziano. 2001. The Internet and education: Findings of the Pew Internet and American Life Project. Pew Internet and American Life Project. http://207.21.232.103/PPF/r/39/report_display.asp.

Levin, Douglas, and Sousan Arafeh. 2002. The digital disconnect: The widening gap between Internet-savvy students and their schools. Pew Internet and American Life Project. http://207.21.232.103/PPF/r/67/report_display.asp.

Levy, David M. 2001. *Scrolling forward: Making sense of documents in the digital age*. New York: Arcade.

Levy, Steven. 2003. A geek bill of rights. *Newsweek*, 8 September, E30.

Lewis, Cynthia, and Bettina Fabos. 2000. But will it work in the heartland? A response and illustration. *Journal of Adolescent and Adult Literacy* 43 (5): 462–69.

Loertscher, David V., and Blanche Woolls. 2002. Teenage users of libraries: A brief overview of the research. *Knowledge Quest* 30 (5): 31–36.

Lueg, Christopher. 2003. Exploring interaction and participation to support information seeking in a social information space. In *From Usenet to CoWebs: Interacting with social information spaces*, ed. Christopher Lueg and Danyel Fisher. London: Springer-Verlag, 232–52.

Luke, Allan. 2003. Foreword to *Literacy in the information age: Inquiries into meaning making with new technologies*, ed. Bertram C. Bruce. Newark, DE: International Reading Association, viii–xi.

Madden, Mary, and Lee Rainie. 2003. America's online pursuits: The changing picture of who's online and what they do. Pew Internet and American Life Project. http://207.21.232.103/PPF/r/106/report_display.asp.

Mann, Thomas. 2003. Why LC subject headings are more important than ever. *American Libraries* 34 (9): 52–54.

Markoff, John, and Edward Wyatt. 2004. Google is adding major libraries to its database. *New York Times*, 14 December, A01.

Meyers, Elaine. 1999. The coolness factor: Ten libraries listen to youth. *American Libraries* 30 (10): 42.

Minkel, Walter. 2003. Going gaga over Google. *School Library Journal* 49 (9): 37.

Moore, Penelope A., and Alison St. George. 1991. Children as information seekers: The cognitive demands of books and library systems. *School Library Media Quarterly* 19 (3): 161–68.

Murray, Bridget. 2000. Reinventing class discussion online. *Monitor on Psychology* 31 (4): 54–56.

Nardi, Bonnie A., and Vicki L. O'Day. 1999. *Information ecologies: Using technology with heart.* Cambridge, MA: MIT Press.

NetDay. 2004. Voices and views of today's tech-savvy students: National report on NetDay Speak Up Day for students 2003. http://www.netday.org/speakupday2003_report.htm.

Neuman, Delia. 1995. High school students' use of databases: Results of a national Delphi study. *Journal of the American Society for Information Science* 46 (4): 284–98.

———. 2003. Research in school library media for the next decade: Polishing the diamond. *Library Trends* 51 (4): 503–24.

Newsweek. 2003. Permanently plugged in, 8 September, E8.

November, Alan C. 1998. Teaching students to fish: Proper use of the Net. *High School Magazine* 6 (1): 22–24.

Nussbaum, Emily. 2004. My so-called blog. *New York Times,* 11 January, 33.

Ostendorf, David. 2001/2002. Christian Identity: An American heresy. *Journal of Hate Studies* 1 (1): 23–55.

Piaget, Jean. 1932. *The moral judgment of the child.* New York: Free Press.

Prensky, Marc. October 2001. Digital natives, digital immigrants. *On the Horizon* 9 (5): 1–6. http://www.marcprensky.com/writing/Prensky%20-%20Digital%20Natives,%20Digital%20Immigrants%20-%20Part1.pdf.

Propaganda Analysis. 1937. How to detect propaganda. 1 (2): 1–4.

Propaganda: How to recognize it and deal with it. Experimental unit of study materials in propaganda analysis for use in junior and senior high schools. 1938. New York: Institute for Propaganda Analysis.

Purdy, Rebecca. 2002. Chat rooms: Teens hanging out on the Web. *Voice of Youth Advocates* 25 (2): 104–5.

Raaijmakers, Jeroen, and Richard M. Schiffrin. 1992. Models for recall and recognition. In *Annual Review of Psychology,* 43. Palo Alto, CA: Annual Reviews, 205–34.

Rainie, Lee, Max Kalehoff, and Dan Hess. 2002. College students and the Web: A Pew Internet data memo. Pew Internet and American Life Project. http://207.21.232.103/PPF/r/73/report_display.asp.

Rawlinson, Nora. 1981. Give 'em what they want! *Library Journal* 106 (20): 2188–90.

Riva, Giuseppe. 2002. The sociocognitive psychology of computer-mediated communication: The present and future of technology-based interactions. *CyberPsychology and Behavior* 5 (6): 581–98.

Sanchez, Claudio. 2004. Debate over whether graphic war images should be used in the classroom as teaching tools. *Weekend All Things Considered.* National Public Radio, 24 May.

Savolainen, Reijo. 1995. Everyday life information seeking: Approaching information seeking in the context of "way of life." *Library and Information Science Research* 17 (3): 259–94.

Simmons, Rachel. 2002. *Odd girl out: The hidden culture of aggression in girls.* Orlando, FL: Harcourt.

———. 2003. Cliques, clicks, bullies and blogs. *Washington Post,* 28 September, B01.

Simon, Herbert A. 1979. *Models of thought.* New Haven, CT: Yale University Press.

Sivin, Jay P., and Ellen R. Bialo. 1992. *Ethical use of information technologies in education: Important issues for America's schools.* Washington, DC: National Institute of Justice, U.S. Department of Justice.

Solomon, Paul. 1993. Children's information retrieval behavior: A case analysis of an OPAC. *Journal of the American Society for Information Science* 44 (5): 245–64.

———. 1994. Children, technology, and instruction: A case study of elementary school children using an online public access catalog (OPAC). *School Library Media Quarterly* 23 (1): 43–51.

Southern Poverty Law Center. Tolerance.org. 2001. Present at the creation. http://www.tolerance.org/news/article_hate.jsp?id=402.

Spink, Amanda, and Charles Cole. 2001. Introduction to the special issue: Everyday life information-seeking research. *Library and Information Science Research* 23 (4): 301–4.

Stripling, Barbara K. 2003. Inquiry-based learning. In *Curriculum connections through the library,* ed. Barbara K. Stripling and Sandra Hughes-Hassell. Westport, CT: Libraries Unlimited, 3–39.

Subrahmanyam, Kaveri, Patricia M. Greenfield, Robert Kraut, and Elisheva Gross. 2002. The impact of computer use on children's and adolescents' development. In *Children in the digital age: Influences of electronic media on development.* Westport, CT: Praeger, 3–33. Also published in *Applied Developmental Psychology* 22 (1): 7–30.

Valenza, Joyce Kasman. 2003a. "Hail, Ranthor!" The rewards of the online gaming world. *Voice of Youth Advocates* 26 (1): 29.

———. 2003b. *Power research tools: Learning activities and posters.* Chicago: American Library Association.

———. 2004. The digital disconnect: The widening gap between Internet-savvy students and their schools. *Knowledge Quest* 32 (4): 50–55.

Van Buren, Cassandra. 2001. Teaching hackers: School computing culture and the future of cyber-rights. *Journal of Information Ethics* 10 (1): 51–72.

Van Der Hoven, Jeroen. 2000. The Internet and varieties of moral wrongdoing. In *Internet Ethics,* ed. Duncan Langford. New York: St. Martin's, 127–57.

VH1 News Special. 2002. Inside hate rock: Examining hatecore music's connection to the white power movement in the U.S., 11 February.

Wallace, Carol McD. 1983. *Should you shut your eyes when you kiss? Or, how to survive "The best years of your life."* Boston: Little, Brown.

Walter, Virginia A. 2003. Public library service to children and teens: A research agenda. *Library Trends* 51 (4): 571–89.

Walter, Virginia A., and Christine L. Borgman. 1991. The Science Library Catalog: A prototype information retrieval system for children. *Journal of Youth Services in Libraries* 4 (2): 159–66.

Walter, Virginia A., and Elaine Meyers. 2003. *Teens and libraries: Getting it right.* Chicago: American Library Association.

Wang, Qingshuo. 2003. Beware of the blog: The possibilities of journalism of the masses. *Voice of Youth Advocates* 26 (1): 28.

Weis, June Pullen. 2004. Contemporary literacy skills: Global initiatives converge. *Knowledge Quest* 32 (4): 12–15.

Willard, Nancy. 1998. Moral development in the information age. In *Proceedings of the Families, Technology, and Education Conference,* Chicago. Also available as ERIC document ED 425 016.

———. 2002. *Computer ethics, etiquette, and safety for the 21st-century student.* Eugene, OR: International Society for Technology in Education.

Williams, Robin. 1990. *The Mac is not a typewriter.* Berkeley, CA: Peachpit.

Wolfson, Paula E., and Lloyd Wolf. 2000. *Jewish mothers: Strength, wisdom, and compassion.* San Francisco: Chronicle Books.

INDEX

Frances Jacobson Harris has been the librarian at University Laboratory High School, University of Illinois at Urbana-Champaign, since 1987. She team-teaches a computer literacy course for eighth- and ninth-grade students that includes a strong focus on information literacy and the ethical use of information and communication technologies. Harris has lectured on topics related to young adults, Internet ethics, and digital information. Her published work has appeared in a range of publications, including the 2004 *Educational Media and Technology Yearbook, School Library Journal, School Library Media Research, Knowledge Quest,* and *Library Trends.* She has a master's degree in library science from the University of Denver.